£5-00
01/08

IMPS OF PROMISE

A History of the King's School, Canterbury

Imps of Promise,
a phrase to describe young scholars used by
JOHN BOYS (1571–1625),
King's Scholar and Dean of Canterbury.

To Clare,
With love from
Freddie, Rosalie and Gwilym.
xxxxxxx

1997.

IMPS OF PROMISE

A History of the King's School, Canterbury

THOMAS HINDE

JAMES
X
JAMES

PICTURE ACKNOWLEDGEMENTS

MOST OF THE PICTURES IN THIS BOOK WERE TAKEN FROM THE SCHOOL AND CATHEDRAL ARCHIVES. THE PUBLISHER AND THE SCHOOL WOULD LIKE TO THANK ANN AND BURY Peerless for their endless enthusiasm and help in photographing archival material and also the Dean and Chapter and their Archivist for their generous cooperation. The publisher and the school are grateful to the following for permission to reproduce material: Ashmolean Museum, Oxford p. 34 (top left); Bodleian Library, University of Oxford ms. Rawl.B.191 fol. 88 p. 2; British Museum p. 9; Canterbury City Museums p. 5; the editors of *The Cantuarian* p. 38; the Lord Mayor and Corporation of Canterbury *Plate 3* (bottom); the Master and Fellows of Corpus Christi College, Cambridge p. 16 (right), p. 21; David Curl p. 108; Mrs Anthony Davenport p. 50; the Dean and Chapter of Canterbury pp. 22, 34 (top right and bottom), 36, 40, 46 and 48; FotoFlite, New Romney, Kent *Plate 1* (bottom); His Grace the Lord Archbishop of Canterbury and the Church Commissioners *Plate 4*; Dr. T. R. Hands, King's School pp. *x*, 50, 56, 104, 111 and 112; Kent County Archives p. 45; the Master and Fellows of Trinity Hall, Cambridge *Plate 2* (bottom); National Portrait Gallery p. 16 (left) and 29; the Owner p. 30; © Ann & Bury Peerless – Slide Resources and Picture Library, Kent p. 10, *Plate 1* (top), *Plate 2* (top), *Plate 5*, *Plate 6*, *Plate 7* (top), *Plate 8*, *Plate 11* and *12*.

Published by James & James (Publishers) Limited, 75 Carleton Road, London N7 0ET
ISBN 0 907383 23 8

First published 1990
Project Editor: Susan Millership Designed by Caroline Archer
Cover design by Ned Hoste, 2H
Cover photograph taken by © Ann & Bury Peerless – Slide Resources and Picture Library
Originated and printed in Great Britain by BAS Printers Limited, Over Wallop, Hampshire
Bound in Great Britain by Hunter & Foulis Limited

ENDPAPERS: *The new Schoolroom and the Norman Staircase in 1855, lithograph by L. L. Razé.*

HALF-TITLE PAGE: *Schoolboy with ball and hockey stick – detail from early 13th century window in the Cathedral.*

TITLE PAGE: *The view over St. Augustine's to the Cathedral drawn by Julian Woodward of the King's School.*

CONTENTS

LIST OF COLOUR PLATES

ACKNOWLEDGEMENTS

I WOULD LIKE FIRST TO ACKNOWLEDGE MY INDEBTEDNESS TO THE AUTHORS OF THE TWO PREVIOUS HISTORIES OF THE KING'S SCHOOL: C. E. WOODRUFF AND H. J. CAPE, 1908, AND THE VERY Reverend D. L. Edwards, 1957. Among the many who have helped me bring the story of the school up-to-date and enabled me to throw a little more light on earlier times I am particularly grateful to John Goudge, Canon Derek Ingram Hill and Alan Wilson for their memories of recent times, Mrs Anthony Davenport for allowing me to use the newly discovered Tylden correspondence, Professor Bryan Keith-Lucas for help with eighteenth-century Kentish history, Dr. B. K. Jeffery for making available his investigations into the Dean and Chapter's records, and Dr. Nigel Ramsay and Mrs (Pamela) Selwyn for providing new material on Master Twyne and his times. Above all I must thank Paul Pollak, the King's School's Archivist. Any merits my book may have are due to his constant help and enthusiastic support.

Thomas Hinde
September 1990

The odd thing is that I can't say I was happy at Canterbury – I was a small, easy-tear-shedding boy – but because I belonged to that school I was rich for evermore with all the history and beauty and tradition that accompanied it.

HUGH WALPOLE

I knew that whatever the war might bring it could never be as bad as the horror of returning to the King's School.

JOCELYN BROOKE

There was a wonderfully cobwebbed feeling about this dizzy and intoxicating antiquity – an ambiance both haughty and obscure which turned famous seats of learning, founded eight hundred or a thousand years later, into gaudy mushrooms . . .

PATRICK LEIGH FERMOR

. . . the only really interesting boy in the House was Patrick Leigh Fermor . . . gifted with an Arthurian and medieval imagination.

ALAN WATTS

It is one of the chief glories of our country that a foundation like this should have continued for over thirteen hundred years . . . Englishmen have never lost sight of certain great aims, of which one is that of education for service.

KING GEORGE VI

FOREWORD

by the Headmaster of the King's School

MY FIRST REACTION ON READING THOMAS HINDE'S HISTORY OF THE KING'S SCHOOL WAS TO MARVEL AT THE SCHOOL'S SURVIVAL FOR NEARLY FOURTEEN HUNDRED YEARS. Its setting at Canterbury – the largest city between London and the Continent, the metropolitical see of England and the site of two of the most important monastic foundations in the land – exposed it starkly to many of the forces that shaped our earlier history. The coming of English Christianity, the flowering of Anglo-Saxon civility, the relapses during the Danish invasions, the Norman Conquest; the Renaissance and the Reformation, the Civil War: all these in turn fostered or threatened the tradition of education at Canterbury that had crystallised in the school. Nor was it later sheltered at Canterbury as the modern world developed, of science and industry, of Empire, world wars and economic transformations. Yet while more powerful institutions have disappeared it approaches its fourteen hundredth birthday brimful of life.

Thomas Hinde had no previous connection with the school when he accepted our invitation to be the author of its latest history. I believe his fresh eye has enabled him to set out the main themes with impartiality and to illuminate them with vivid and amusing detail, much of it arising from the school's post-Reformation links with the Cathedral and its Precincts. Inevitably he has shared much of the material of his predecessors: but his interpretations are very much his own and he has also been able to include material discovered more recently, such as the Tylden letters between 18th century King's Scholars or what Marlowe's headmaster, John Gresshop, had in his remarkable library. His account of the school over the last 30 to 40 years, under Dr Shirley and his successors, overlaps only slightly with previously published accounts and assessments.

I am confident that *Imps of Promise* will prove to be not only a highly readable account of the school for all its friends but also a distinctive contribution to English educational and social history.

Anthony Phillips
October 1990

New uses for old places.

I

ST AUGUSTINE TO HENRY VIII

THE KING'S SCHOOL, CANTERBURY, IS ENGLAND'S OLDEST SCHOOL – SO THE HISTORIAN ARTHUR LEACH CLAIMED IN A LETTER TO *THE TIMES* IN 1896. ABANDONING HIS SUPPORT for St Peter's School, York, and rejecting the claims of Rochester, Dunwich, and St Paul's, London, he firmly stated that a school was started by St Augustine when he came to Canterbury in 597 to bring back Christianity from Rome. During the last 100 years no one has directly contradicted Leach's claim, but they have nibbled at its edges, asking in particular what the word 'school' means when used about an English institution of the late sixth century.

The reason for uncertainty is that the evidence is circumstantial or by analogy. It can persuasively be argued that, since Christianity did not return to England from Ireland and the West, where it had survived from Roman times, but came direct from Rome, and since it therefore brought with it a ritual and holy books written in Latin, among the first things Augustine must have needed to do was to teach Latin to the converts who were to become his English priests and clerks. But circumstantial arguments of this sort are supported by little that is concrete.

What there is comes largely from the Venerable Bede's *Ecclesiastical History*. Though Bede wrote some 130 years later (c.731), he has a good reputation for reliability. He makes it clear that Englishmen were indeed soon becoming priests. In 644 Archbishop Honorius consecrated Ithamar, 'born in Kent but as polished and learned as his predecessors'. In 655 Ithamar consecrated Deusdedit, a West Saxon, sixth Archbishop of Canterbury, and Deusdedit in turn consecrated Damian, a South Saxon, to succeed Ithamar.

More significantly Bede writes that in 631 King Sigbert of East Anglia, a 'good and religious man' who had been baptized when in exile in France, 'on his return to his own country . . . wishing without delay to imitate such things as he had seen well managed in France . . . established a school in which boys might be brought up to letters. In this he enjoyed the help of Bishop Felix, whom he had received from Kent, who supplied for them schoolmasters and lecturers in the Kentish manner.'

The question which must be asked is whether these teachers came from Kent in general or from Canterbury in particular. In favour of Canterbury, Leach argues that the word used by Bede – *Cantuariorum* – could mean 'of Canterbury' as well as 'of Kent'. But elsewhere when Bede means Canterbury he calls it *Doruvernum* (a variant of its usual Roman name, *Durovernum*), so the translation 'of Kent' must be correct. The best argument remains a circumstantial one: if by 631 there were educational establishments at more than one place in Kent, the most likely to have been founded first and have teachers to spare would have been Canterbury. Rochester, the only other Kentish see, was bishopless around 630 and not functioning well.

The question of the origin of Sigbert's teachers has been discussed for at least 400 years. In the sixteenth century the learned John Twyne – headmaster both before and after its refounding by Henry VIII (he will be fully described later) – noted alongside a mediaeval retelling of Bede's story (in Higden's *Polychronicon*), 'de schola Cantuar': 'of Canterbury school'. Twyne was an antiquary who did not make casual guesses and he apparently believed they came from the actual school of which he was the master.

At around the time that East Anglia was receiving educational help from Kent, probably from Canterbury, one James the Deacon was extending Canterbury's influence to York. Here James, 'as the numbers of the faithful recovered began to train many in the Roman, or Kentish, method of chanting'. Kentish church singing was already, it seems, famous, and must have been taught at some educational institution there.

In 669 Theodore of Tarsus arrived in England to be the new Archbishop of Canterbury. Theodore is the first archbishop who presided for certain over a school at Canterbury. He was a remarkable man, aged 66 when appointed; at a time when life was short he must have seemed old indeed. With him came the North African, Hadrian, abbot of a monastery near Naples, who soon became abbot of the monastery which St Augustine had founded at Canterbury alongside his cathedral church, at first called St Peter and St Paul's, eventually St Augustine's. About Theodore and Hadrian Bede writes, 'And because they were deeply learned both in scripture and in secular writings the hearts of the company of pupils that had gathered about them were daily refreshed with streams of sound knowledge.

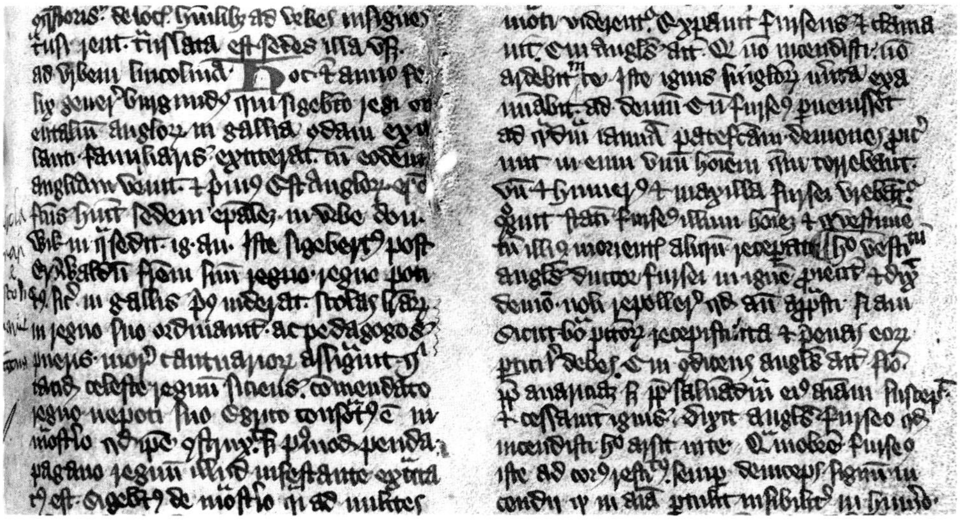

John Twyne's marginal gloss 'de schola Cantuar' connects his Canterbury School with the Kentish educators of AD 631.

Together with the finest parts of scripture they passed on to their hearers the arts of quantity, of astronomy, and of calculating the calendar. This is shown by some of their pupils yet living who know Latin and Greek as well as they know their own mother tongue.

'Not since the English had settled in Britain were there happier times than then. Kings both powerful and Christian overawed the conspiring barbarians while the solemn hopes of all looked to the joys of the heavenly kingdom so newly made known to them. Whoever wished to become grounded in reading scripture had ready access to masters for instruction.'

Other scraps of evidence confirm the attention given to education by Theodore and Hadrian. A letter written by St Aldhelm, first Bishop of Sherborne, speaks of Hadrian as 'the venerated teacher of my rude infancy'. And in a letter to the Bishop of Winchester Aldhelm writes that he has been kept at Canterbury during Christmas, studying Roman law, verse making and music, arithmetic and astronomy. It seems clear that, some 70 years after St Augustine's arrival, there was a school at Canterbury teaching subjects which were not purely theological. Bede's enthusiastic description of this school implies a contrast with earlier times. Had a school of this sort already existed he would surely have said so. Against this must be balanced the arguments already given, that within 35 years of Augustine's arrival, Kentish teaching had acquired a reputation which extended to East Anglia and Kentish chanting to York. The conclusion must be that there was indeed education of some sort going on at Canterbury from about 600, but that its curriculum was memorably extended by Theodore and Hadrian.

During the 400 years which followed the death of Theodore in 690 all becomes obscure again. In these centuries the Kingdom of Wessex grew in importance while Kent declined. But Alcuin (c.732–804), master of the school at York and educational adviser to Charlemagne, confirms Canterbury's continuing cultural importance, writing that there 'the most radiant torches of Britain have their resting place . . . whence the light of truth has spread through all the land'. A school must surely have been at the centre of this light of truth, as it must have been when St Dunstan was archbishop (959–88) – he came from Glastonbury with a reputation as a teacher.

From 790 onwards Kent was continually invaded by Norsemen and Danes, their attacks culminating in the Danish raid of 1011 when they kidnapped and murdered Archbishop Alphege. In spite of such events, an illustration of the early fifteenth century shows, set centrally on the altar of St Augustine's Abbey, books which probably include the actual Gospels which Pope Gregory sent to St Augustine soon after his arrival at Canterbury. This book is now at Corpus Christi College, Cambridge, what is probably another in the Bodleian, Oxford. Not only does their place of honour suggest the importance of education in the early church at Canterbury, but their survival suggests that none of the Danish raids can have been as destructive of the city and its institutions as the archbishop's murder makes them sound.

The subjects studied by students at Canterbury in Theodore's time are given by Bede as Latin, Greek, the Bible, arithmetic, and astronomy. At York, Alcuin, describing a time some 50 years later, writes about Albert, his master at the school there, 'To some he diligently gave the art of the Science of Grammar, pouring into others the streams of Rhetoric. These he polished on the grindstone of law, those he taught to sing in Aeonian chant, instructing others to play on the pipe of Castaly and to run over the ridges of Parnassus with lyric feet: others the aforesaid Master caused to know the harmony of the sky and of the sun, the labours of the moon, the five belts of the heavens, the seven wandering stars, their rising and their setting – the tides and earthquake, the natures of men, cattle, birds, and wild beasts, the divers kinds of number and various figures. He gave certainty to Easter's return and especially did he unveil the mysteries of Holy Scripture . . .'.

It is sometimes suggested that subjects like astronomy and arithmetic were studied only for religious reasons. In his collection of Alcuin's letters, Stephen Allott writes, 'The religious interest was dominant throughout. Astronomy, for example, was used for the understanding of the church calendar and arithmetic for applying numerical allegories to the Scriptures.' But Alcuin's description implies that they were also studied as part of a general pursuit of knowledge. His list, indeed, makes the subjects Albert taught sound like both the mediaeval trivium (grammar, rhetoric, and logic) and the quadrivium (arithmetic, geometry, music, and astronomy) with some science and natural history thrown in.

At some time probably towards the end of this period there began to be monks as well as secular clergy at Christ Church Cathedral, Canterbury. Since there were monks, there was almost certainly a school for novices, but as Christ Church was not yet the priory it became under the Normans, novice and grammar schools may have been one and the same. The earliest tales which give the flavour of school life at Canterbury were perhaps describing such a school.

They are in fact probably a single tale, told first at the end of the eleventh century by the monk Osbern in his life of St Dunstan, given more miraculous twists by another monk, Eadmer. In the original version a young girl recovers her sight as a result of spending the night by St Dunstan's tomb. Next morning the boys of the school parade for their regular punishments, but the masters are persuaded to excuse them on the grounds that they should be as merciful as St Dunstan has just been. In subsequent Osbern versions St Dunstan himself appears to one of the boys, puts the masters to sleep, and asks the boy in return to have the infant son of Earl Harold (as the Normans called the late king) removed from the neighbourhood of his tomb where its smell is offending him. Finally Eadmer makes the punishment an annual one, administered five days before Christmas as part of the Advent penance, adds that it was no mere light caning but a thorough scourging with whips of knotted bull's hide, and makes St Dunstan appear a second time and tell the provost that if the unbaptized child is not removed the cathedral will burn down – a forecast duly fulfilled in 1067.

Despite the fairytale quality of these monkish tales they are important evidence that there was a well-established school at Canterbury immediately before the Norman Conquest. Even if Norman chroniclers were inclined to exaggerate the brutality of Saxon times, Osbern and Eadmer probably give an idea of the sort of treatment an eleventh-century schoolboy at Canterbury could expect.

Where, then, was the schoolroom of this school? Eadmer says that it was in the north tower of the old cathedral. Woodruff and Cape, in their 1908 history

Canterbury from the North as it appeared in about 1170. The Green Court with the Norman Staircase, the Mint Yard and the courtyard where the Shirley Hall now stands are already clearly established. St Augustine's is too far East to appear. (Canterbury Heritage Museum ©)

of the school, guess that it stood on the site of the old timbered building across the road from the Mint Yard Gate, but admit that their suggestion is only based on eighteenth-century ideas about where St Augustine's first house stood, and on the assumption that the school would have been there too. The fact is that we don't know, and a better guess is that during the seven centuries when it can't be located it was probably in more than one place.

Another two centuries of uncertainty about education at Canterbury follow the Norman Conquest, but there are more clues, and these ironically have led to a better defined disagreement between the King's School's two twentieth-century historians.

The main events of the time are clear enough: the arrival of the Norman Archbishop Lanfranc in 1070 and the murder of Thomas Becket in 1170. Lanfranc found the cathedral still a ruin from the fire of 1067. Within seven years he had built a magnificent new one in Norman style and established it as the church of a Benedictine priory ruled by a prior – though he, as archbishop, was its abbot. Lanfranc's 'constitutions' for the priory refer to the teaching of boys in what seems to be an elementary school, and Woodruff and Cape (1908) argue that, because no mention is made of a more advanced school, there must already have been a well-established one. Lanfranc himself had been a noted teacher of grammar and theology in his previous position at the Abbey of Bec in France.

Edwards (1957), on the other hand, argues that a charter of the Church of St Gregory outside the North Gate of the city, giving its canons the right to establish a school of grammar and music, shows that it was here rather than at the cathedral that Lanfranc wished to establish a grammar school for the people of the city and neighbourhood. But if so, it is surprising that there is not a single further mention in any records of a school at St Gregory's.

To complicate the educational scene at Canterbury in the late eleventh and twelfth centuries, there would have now certainly been novice schools both at Christ Church Priory and at St Augustine's Abbey. And from 1320 there are references to yet another school, the school of the Almonry. The Almonry was the centre from which the monks distributed charity, and stood in the Mint Yard where, by 1328, it had its own chapel. The school which the monks ran here would admit only boys over ten who could already sing and read. There are various subsequent mentions of the customs and the masters of the Almonry School. Between 1509 and 1525 we know the names of nine pupils there, from charitable grants made to them by the prior.

But almost a century before we first hear of an Almonry School there was a schoolhouse at Canterbury. In 1224, according to the Franciscan friar, Thomas Eccleston (c.1258), nine of his order came to the city from the Continent. These were the first Greycoat friars to reach England – the order had only obtained papal approval for its revised rule in 1223. They came, of course, without money. Four of the group soon went on to London to present their letters of recommendation to Henry III. The other five remained at Canterbury where they were lodged by the 'Master of the Poor Priests' Hospice' in a small room below the school. All day they had to stay there, but when school ended they were able to climb to the schoolroom itself, warm themselves by a fire and drink the dregs of the small beer which the scholars had left, each in turn at the same time making some *verba aedificationis* ('edifying remark'). Woodruff and Cape have no doubt that this schoolhouse was the premises of the Archbishop's School, but Edwards argues that, because it was under the control of the Master of the Poor Priests' Hospice, it must have belonged to some other Canterbury school.

Whatever the truth, there is no doubt that, 35 years later, the Archbishop's School existed. For the first time (1259) we hear of a citizen of Canterbury known as the 'Rector of the Schools of the City of Canterbury'. His name, 'Master Robert', is one in a list of Canterbury citizens appended to an appeal by the Prior of Christ Church to the Roman Curia against Archbishop Boniface who, the prior claimed, had interfered in the priory's affairs where he had no right to. Robert's title, 'master', shows that he was a layman and that he had a licence to teach from the cathedral chancellor or from some university, but nothing more is known of him.

Two more masters of the Archbishop's School are known during the next 50 years, but it is only with the appointment of John Everard in 1310 that we come to one who is more than a name. Everard's behaviour is of the greatest interest for it shows that during the first half of the fourteenth century the masters of the school claimed remarkable powers, and suggests that at this time the school had some of the characteristics of a university.

Everard had in his school a peculiarly difficult and litigious student named

PLATE 1
Top: Canterbury Cathedral and St. Augustine's Abbey from the East. Their founder St. Augustine, and his companions, entered the city near here in AD 597.

Bottom: Canterbury from the West. Many School buildings are grouped North of the Cathedral about the Green Court, the Mint Yard and the courtyard of the old Archbishop's Palace.

PLATE 2

St. John of Beverley and St. Aldhelm, two early Canterbury scholars, from a stained glass window in the Memorial Chapel.

The books sent by Pope Gregory to St. Augustine, in a place of honour on the high altar of St. Augustine's Abbey.

Richard Hall, so much so that this young man must surely have been more than a mere teenager. Soon after Everard's appointment Hall attacked the school's lower master, and when summoned to appear before Everard to defend himself refused to attend. Everard excommunicated him. Hall now went to the Archbishop's Court of Arches, claiming that the master had no power to excommunicate. The Commissary of the See of Canterbury, however, informed the court that he had seen the master's authority and furthermore that according to various trustworthy clerks and laymen the master had had this power for more than 40 years.

The court seems not to have been convinced and while it hesitated Hall applied to the King's Court. When he missed his day at court he claimed that he had been unable to attend because he was imprisoned by the archbishop's chancellor. Nevertheless, he obtained from the Sheriff of Kent a writ requiring the bailiffs to attach both headmaster Everard and the commissary for pursuing the case in the wrong court.

Meanwhile, Everard made further complaints against Hall, accusing him among other things of continuing to take the Sacrament though excommunicated, of boasting of his immorality, of suborning false witnesses, and of a further assault. Eventually, two years from the start of the affair, Hall was absolved, but whether because he proved himself in the right or because he submitted we do not know.

The following year (1314) another student, Thomas of Birchwood, also assaulted the school's lower master, but instead of excommunicating him Everard held a court of the school to decide how he should be treated. This case is interesting because some of the members of the school court are described as bachelors, a term applied at the time to scholars who had completed four years of university studies. Canterbury, it seems, was already awarding its scholars this qualification, yet it was not till four years later that Cambridge University was officially licensed by the Pope. It must, however, be admitted that Canterbury's bachelors may have been merely Bachelors of Grammar, a lower degree than that of Bachelor of Arts.

During his remaining years as the school's master, Everard was involved in two cases of equal significance, since in these he claimed power not merely over his scholars, but over members of the general public who had come into conflict with them. In one he prohibited Roger the lime-burner from attending church because he had assaulted a student, in the other a woman, Joan Modi, admitted a similar assault and was given a day on which to appear for her sentence. Powers of this sort were only granted to the Chancellor of Oxford in 1275 and at Cambridge not until many years later.

By 1321 Ralph of Waltham had succeeded Everard and that year he was engaged in significant proceedings of another kind: an attempt to restrict the size of a rival school. This was being conducted by Robert de Henry, Rector of St Martin's, who had the right to enrol an unlimited number of junior boys but only thirteen for grammar-school education. To ensure that this rule was kept, Ralph of Waltham would send his lower master to make inspections, but now complained to the archbishop that Robert would hide boys during these checks. Ralph was found to be in the right and the archbishop threatened to excommunicate Robert if he continued to enrol more students than thirteen. Ralph's action clearly suggests that he received fees from his students and was for this reason keen to restrict the size of a rival school. There is, indeed, no evidence that the mediaeval Archbishop's School ever gave free education, though from time to time it gave charitable grants to certain poor boys.

Why, it may be asked, if the Archbishop's School at this time had some of the characteristics of a university did it not grow into one? The Black Death (1349) provides a possible answer. Many died at Canterbury – but Oxford and Cambridge suffered too. A more likely explanation is that the school was too closely under the control of the Church in the form of the archbishop and priory ever to have the independence a university required. Neither Oxford nor Cambridge had even a bishop in the Middle Ages.

During the fifteenth century there are two tantalizingly brief scraps of information about the school; a letter from the prior to the archbishop written some time between 1472 and 1486 shows that the school was still keenly maintaining its monopoly on local education. The prior asks 'your good faderhode' to 'send doun your commaundment that noon othir perticuler scole be kept nygh by'. Either the archbishop ignored the prior's request or understood that the Almonry School was an exception. In the same letter the prior asks the archbishop's help with restoring the schoolhouse which was 'ruynous and evill repaired'.

In 1464 the Christ Church monk, John Stone, mentions a custom which brings the school more vividly to life than anything since the tales of the monks Osbern and Eadmer. That year on St Nicholas's Day (6 December) the school's masters had failed to appoint a boy-bishop. Boy-bishops were customarily chosen on this day in most cathedrals with attached schools and indeed in many parishes. They held their office at least until the Feast of the Innocents, three weeks later.

During their time in office boy-bishops preached, processed, and, in general, carried out the duties of the bishop (officiating at High Mass excepted). There is no evidence that they parodied their superiors, indeed they seem to have had real importance. They were entitled to choose new prebendaries, and if a boy-bishop died while in office he was buried in his episcopal ornaments with the full ceremony due to a bishop. In about 1675 the tomb of a boy-bishop was found at Salisbury. A procession led by a small boy in bishop's mitre, carrying bishop's crozier, followed by other small boys dressed as priests, all carrying burning tapers and chanting, no doubt in itself seemed quaint and gave the performers an opportunity to mock as well as imitate their adult equivalents, but at a time when all drama was religious it probably had the nature of a straight play rather than a satirical review.

Though the custom was considered Popish and was suppressed at the Reformation, it was revived under Queen Mary. John Strype's description of 1556 suggests that the bishop and his followers had by then acquired the character of a carol-singing party. 'St. Nicholas', he writes, '. . . went abroad in most parts of London, singing after the old fashion, and was received with many ignorant but well-disposed people into their houses, and had as much good cheer as ever was wont to be had before.' No doubt similar singing parties had been traditional at Canterbury. The whole ritual was perhaps something of a fiesta, making a welcome break in monastic routine, and the fact that the monk, John Stone, recorded the masters' names and their failure shows how serious a lapse theirs had been.

In other ways the customs, domestic arrangements, and curriculum of the Archbishop's School were probably similar to those of its contemporaries. The dormitories would have been basic – at Wells scholars slept three to a bed, two small boys with their heads at the top end, one bigger boy with his head between their feet. And no doubt at Canterbury as at Wells they were encouraged to develop polite table manners: to cut their bread with a knife rather than gnaw at it, to drink with their mouths empty, to refrain from eating ravenously, and not to pick their teeth with their knives.

Thomas Linacre drawn by an unknown French artist.

They would have worked long hours – at Wells they had only half an hour's play time a day – and Latin would have been the most important subject. They would have read mediaeval Latin authors. John of Salisbury, Bishop of Chartres (who visited Canterbury in 1147 and was considered one of the most learned men of his time) had not read Caeser, Tacitus, Plautus, Lucretius, nor even the odes of Horace – which later became such a central feature of the King's School's teaching. The Greek which Archbishop Theodore had taught his students to speak like their native language had long been dropped. The first Greek lectures at Oxford were not given till 1465 and the first Greek teacher, William Grocyn, not appointed till 1491.

One of those who helped bring the new humanism from Italy (and was a close friend of Grocyn's) was Thomas Linacre. Linacre was probably born near Dover and attended the Archbishop's School in about 1472, his patron being Prior William Selling. It was Selling who recommended him to Oxford where he became a fellow of All Souls, and who then took him to Italy. There he lived in the house of Lorenzo de' Medici at Florence, studied Greek in other cities, and became interested in medicine at Padua. Back in England he taught Greek to Sir Thomas More and Erasmus and became tutor to Prince Arthur, Henry VIII's elder brother who would have become king instead of Henry if he had survived. He was also physician to Prince Henry, though not an entirely successful one by modern standards, whichever of the complaints (scurvy, osteomyelitis or syphilis) Henry in fact suffered from. Nevertheless, it was as a physician that Linacre was best known in his day. He founded and was first president of the Royal College of Physicians, and translated medical books from Greek and Latin into English. Today one of the school's houses is named after him.

Four years before he died, Linacre eventually became a priest, and so, almost certainly, did most of the school's scholars in the Middle Ages. Two became Archbishops of Canterbury. Archbishop Robert of Winchelsea was much involved in national politics, resisting Edward I's demands that the clergy should pay taxes. During this controversy the lay fees of the Province of Canterbury were confiscated and the clergy of the country outlawed. In the following reign Robert was one of those who deplored Edward II's homosexual relationship with the young French knight, Piers Gaveston. A century and a half later, John Kemp, 'son of a poor husbandman' of Kent, rose in succession to be Bishop of Rochester and of London, Archbishop of York, then of Canterbury and a cardinal (1452–4). Before Henry VI came of age, Kemp was a member of the Council of Regency.

One other person must be mentioned from these centuries: Meister (Master) Omer. There is no evidence that he was educated at the Archbishop's School

Linacre House – once the canonical residence of Nelson's brother – is one of the School's thirteen Houses.

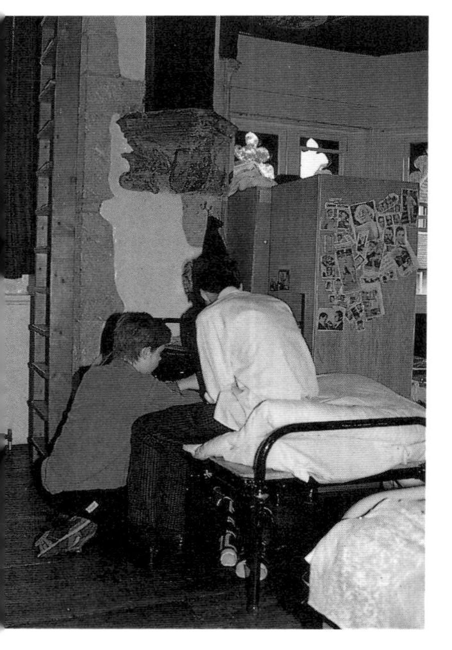

Corbels and cassettes in Meister Omers. This House has borne Master Omer's name for over six centuries.

(though it seems quite possible) but on the document of 1259 which carries the name of the first known master of the school, Omer's name also appears, as a legal official of the archbishop's. He held this position for 31 years from 1249 to 1280, and it was then that he probably occupied or built what has since become Meister Omers, another of the school's boarding houses. After Omer's time it was used for the prior's chief guests, and was much extended by Thomas Chillenden, prior 1391 to 1411. It contains the great fireplace which is believed to have the largest span of any in England (21 feet 8 inches). The entrance hall is decorated with the arms of Queen Elizabeth, suggesting that she may have been entertained here.

There is little doubt why the Archbishop's School thrived in mediaeval times. Not only was it supported by one of the country's most prosperous monasteries, but it provided education for a city which, after Becket's murder, contained the country's most visited pilgrim shrine. In the fifteenth century, though fewer pilgrims came, Canterbury continued to grow. From Roman times it had been the most important place on the road between London and the Continent, the junction of roads to four important ports. Throughout the Middle Ages it was a stopping place for most of the country's foreign visitors and as a result supported a more sophisticated society than any other provincial town in the country. It was the children of this society that the Archbishop's School educated.

2

OLD FAITH AND NEW

THE LAST HEAD OF THE ARCHBISHOP'S SCHOOL WAS MASTER JOHN TWYNE – A LAYMAN, LIKE THE FIRST KNOWN HEAD, MASTER ROBERT, SOME 300 YEARS EARLIER. THE HEADMASTER OF the new King's School, established by Henry VIII after the dissolution of the Priory of Christ Church along with the rest of the country's monasteries was the same John Twyne. Twyne held the two positions for more than 35 years, from about 1524 to about 1560. He was a remarkable man, probably the most remarkable for his scholarship and public positions of all the school's headmasters, but his survival through these revolutionary times is still surprising. How did it come about?

Christ Church Priory was the last of the country's monastic institutions to go. When it was visited by Dr Layton and his commissioners they found none of the self-indulgence and loose living which they discovered elsewhere and the only dramatic event of their visit was a fire (which destroyed many of the late Prior Selling's valuable books) started, according to John Leland, by the commissioners' drunken servants. In March 1540 the monks of Christ Church were forced to surrender, but they were treated so considerately that, although Prior Goldwell did not become the new dean (he wrote to Thomas Cromwell claiming the position) he was allowed to retire on a pension. So were most of his monks. Six, however, became prebendaries under the Statutes of the new collegiate body.

These six, together with six more prebendaries and the dean himself, formed the cathedral's new Governing Body. The Statutes then listed the remainder of the cathedral's establishment. It was to include 'two Public Teachers of the boys in Grammar and fifty boys to be instructed in Grammar'. Canterbury's allowance of scholars was generous; among similar schools of the time Westminster was allowed 40 and Durham 18.

Statute 27 describes the school which the new master and lower master were to run. The 50 scholars were to be selected by an entrance exam, taken when they were between nine and 15 years old, which would qualify them to be educated free at the school for four years. Dull boys could be expelled; on the other hand, any selected by the dean and headmaster could stay for an extra year – called the 'Year of Grace'.

The scholars were to be poor (*pauperes et amicorum ope destituti*). Some of the commissioners who drafted the Statutes opposed this condition, arguing, according to a letter from Cranmer's secretary, Ralph Morice, that the school should be for the sons of gentlemen, since 'husbandmen's children . . . were more meet . . . for the plough and to be artificers . . .'. Against this Cranmer argued that on their own the children of the best born were liable to 'become unapt to learn and very dolts, as I myself have seen no small number of them very dull and without all manner of capacity', while 'the poor man's son by painstaking for the most part will be learned'. He agreed, however, that 'if the gentleman's son be apt to learning let him be admitted', and there is little doubt that the scholars of the new school were mostly sons of the gentry.

The school is described in more detail in Statute 41, a statute which survives in the Bodleian Library's manuscript but not in the cathedral's copy. This adds that to be admitted a boy must be able to read, and to recite in the vernacular the Lord's Prayer, the Angelic Salutation, the Apostles' Creed, and the Ten Commandments – improbable achievements for a genuinely poor boy. The school was to be divided into six (or five) classes, the lower three to be taught by the lower master, the top three by the headmaster. But the headmaster was to visit every class once, twice, or three times a week to test the boys, to encourage friends to remove those 'wholly unfit for letters' and, three times a year, to promote deserving boys from class to class.

In the bottom class they were to learn English, in the second to start Latin and read among other things Aesop's *Fables*. In the third class they were to reach a standard in Latin 'so that no noun or verb be found anywhere which they do not know how to inflect in every detail'. In the fifth class they were to learn the rules for writing Latin verse and speeches. In the top class they were to read Horace and Cicero, and to 'acquire the faculty of speaking Latin, so far as is possible for boys'. Indeed, they were to speak to each other only in Latin or Greek, both in school and at play.

Each evening between 6 and 7 o'clock they were to repeat what they had learned that day to more advanced students, in the presence of 'several masters'. There is no suggestion that the more advanced students were to have the authority of monitors, and the fact that masters were to be present suggests the opposite.

In their play time the scholars were not to practise 'any games which are not of a gentlemanly appearance and free of all lowness', and they were to play *together* to prevent them from 'wandering about here and there', and incurring 'some loss of character . . .'.

Statute 30 described the feeding arrangements for the junior members of the cathedral's establishment. There were to be three dining tables. The headmaster was to sit at the first (under the precentor), the lower master at the next, and the students and choristers at the third. The dining hall stood between today's Cathedral Library and the Green Court, where a small fragment of it can still be seen in the vaults behind Lardergate. The rest was destroyed in Commonwealth times.

Statute 31 requires that before Christmas each year a scholar should be given an allowance of cloth for his purple gown so that he could celebrate the festival with new clothes as well as new spirits. Then and throughout the year scholars and masters were to play a part in the cathedral services which by today's standards occupied a remarkable amount of their time. Every day they were to attend High Mass in the cathedral and to stay there until the choristers had finished their singing of the *Angus Dei*, meditating on Psalms 51 and 67 or saying to themselves certain listed prayers. On Sundays and Feast days they were to attend Matins, Processions, and Vespers (in clean surplices). In the school itself there were to be morning prayers presided over by the lower master at 6 a.m. and evening prayers at 5 p.m.

The Statutes allotted each scholar, for his food and in kind, £4 a year, a generous sum at the time. The headmaster's salary of £20 and the lower master's of £10 seem less generous when compared with those of contemporary schoolmasters and this may explain the rapid turnover of lower masters. During the following hundred years there were no fewer than nineteen. They undoubtedly supplemented their salaries by charging for teaching; the accounts of the Dean and Chapter confirm that commoners were now learning and eating alongside the 50 scholars.

The new school was probably in practice the old school refounded. At the time of the Dissolution there were a number of schools at Canterbury of which the Archbishop's was the most important. After the Dissolution these schools were replaced by the King's School. It is unlikely that the King's School would have enrolled an entirely new batch of scholars, and equally unlikely that previous scholars would have been dismissed without further education.

The new school may also have enrolled some of the novices of the priory's novice school. On a list of the monks at the time of the Dissolution the word 'scholar' appears alongside nine names. Unfortunately, these 'scholars' are only given their monkish names, so it is impossible to identify them among the King's School's first 50 scholars – who are, of course, listed by their proper names. At least one was beyond school age and probably so described because he became an Oxford or Cambridge scholar. But others may well have been among the scholars of the refounded school.

About the reappearance of John Twyne as headmaster there is no doubt, and this is the strongest evidence of continuity. Twyne was educated at Oxford, but by 1540 had been at Canterbury for about 16 years. According to Anthony Wood's *Athenae Oxonienses*, 1691, when Twyne left Oxford he became 'supreme Moderator of the Free-School within the cemetery at Canterbury' where he 'grew rich'. By 1532, if not before, he was living at St Augustine's Abbey.

It was perhaps while living at the abbey that he drafted his only published book, *De Rebus Albionicis, Britannicis atque Anglicis* . . . (though he certainly revised it later and it was only published by his son in 1590 after his death). It is set at Sturry Court, then a manor of the abbey's, now by coincidence the Junior King's School, and takes the form of a symposium, with John Foche, the abbey's last abbot, and John Dygon, the last prior, as two of the main speakers. The other is Nicholas Wotton, the future Dean of Canterbury, while Twyne himself intervenes occasionally.

These four raise all manner of questions, but discuss at greatest length the early history of Britain. Twyne's index of the 87 authors he consulted, including a number whose work then existed only in manuscript, shows that history was his main interest and that he was one of the first historians to compare carefully written evidence and reject the legends of unreliable chroniclers like William of

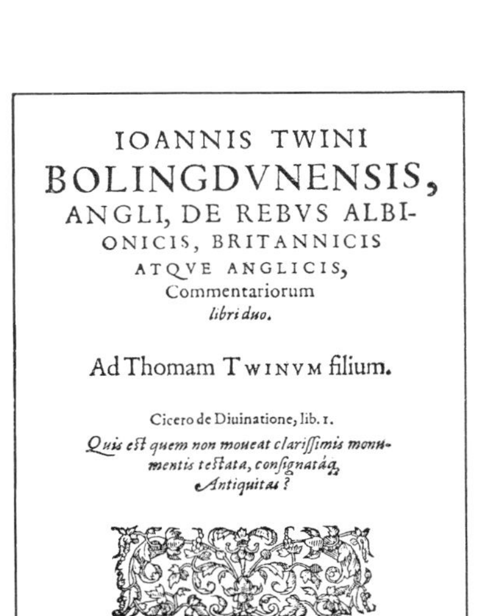
IOANNIS TWINI
BOLINGDVNENSIS,
ANGLI, DE REBVS ALBIONICIS, BRITANNICIS
ATQVE ANGLICIS,
Commentariorum
libri duo.

Ad Thomam TWINVM filium.

Cicero de Diuinatione, lib. I.
Quis est quem non moueat clarissimis monumentis testata, consignataq; Antiquitas?

LONDINI,
Excudebat Edm. Bollifantus, pro
Richardo Watkins.
1590

Twyne planned a number of works but only the De Rebus *was finished (or has survived). His Hampshire origins at Bullingdon are the occasion of a gentle tease by his Kentish friends in the book.*

Malmesbury. He dismisses once and for all the story that a band of Trojans led by Brutus were our first colonists (so explaining the name Britain) and substitutes the Phoenicians. True, he makes them interbreed with the original inhabitants, descendents of Albion, son of Neptune, but it was nevertheless a good guess, based on recent suggestions by the scholar, John Vives, that the Phoenicians had come to south-west Spain for minerals. If they reached Spain, Twyne argues, they probably came to England for Cornish tin. His supporting evidence is more curious. English moustaches and Welsh women's traditional dresses, he claims to be examples of Phoenician influence. And woad was the cosmetic they used to keep themselves swarthy when they grew pale in the English climate. Some of the other matters he considers are equally fantastic, for example a shower of frogs which he and Wotton had recently experienced south of Canterbury on Barham Down. But Twyne's attempt at the early history of Britain, which includes the suggestion that it was once joined to the Continent, makes him 'one of the most original antiquarians of the 16th century . . . a hundred years ahead of his time'.

His residence at St Augustine's and friendship with its abbot and prior have been seen as confirmation that Twyne, throughout his life, was a Catholic reactionary. But there is evidence that at this time he was, on the contrary, an active Protestant sympathizer. In 1534 he was sent twice in a week by Cranmer to Sandwich to 'read a lecture of heresy' (meaning protestantism to the monkish writer). Two years later he appears in two presentments for heresy prepared for the city's quarter sessions. In the first he and others are accused of speaking much against the worshipping of saints and against the usages of the Holy Church. In the second he is accused of abetting a Canterbury printer who was printing and selling books which were against the faith of true Christians.

Later in his life Twyne was a good friend of the royal printer, Reyner Wolfe. Wolfe was a well-known Protestant, and had been brought from Germany to England by Cranmer (whose second wife was German) before 1537. It is possible that Cranmer introduced him to Twyne at this time. Whether he did or not, Twyne was apparently an active protester against the old faith in the 1530s.

It is also an oversimplification, to put it mildly, to imply when trying to explain Twyne's reappointment as headmaster, that those who reappointed him were of one religious persuasion. Archbishop Cranmer and various of the prebendaries certainly weren't, as the so-called Plot of the Prebendaries of 1542–3 showed. By this time the Six Articles had been passed by Parliament, reasserting many Catholic doctrines, including transubstantiation and the celibacy of priests, demonstrating that Henry VIII, once free from the Pope, was anxious not to offend further his Catholic subjects. The prebendaries plotted to reveal the Protestant extremism of Cranmer and so have him disgraced, but the king proved loyal to Cranmer, the plot failed, and several of them were sent to prison.

The real explanation of Twyne's reappointment probably has less connection either with his religious views or with those of the cathedral's governing body than with his personal friendships and his standing as a citizen of Canterbury. Cranmer had used him and must have trusted him. Wotton, the new dean, was a close friend, as *De Rebus Albionicis* subsequently showed. It is true that Wotton was less of a churchman than a diplomat, indeed one of Henry VIII's most trusted diplomats. Though he was involved in obtaining the painting of Anne of Cleves by Holbein which so unfortunately persuaded Henry VIII that he could bear to marry the lady, Henry sent him to break the news of the divorce to Anne's brother, the Duke of Cleves, and continued to trust him. Absentee from Canterbury as Wotton often was, his friendship cannot have harmed Twyne.

Just as significantly, Twyne had by now married Alice Piper, daughter of a freeman of Canterbury, which entitled Twyne himself in 1538 to become a freeman of the city. By 1540 he was a member of the Common Council.

Twyne's position as master of the King's School did not prevent him from continuing to play the part of an important citizen of Canterbury. In 1544–5 he was sheriff of the city, and in 1553 he became an alderman, and Canterbury's Member of Parliament. During Edward VI's reign, however, he was summoned to London where he was imprisoned in the Tower. This is the first evidence that he was now in trouble for being on the opposite, Catholic side. Protestant feelings at the time were at their most extreme, in Canterbury cathedral services began to be read in English, and figures of saints, frescoes, tapestries, and chantry chapels were destroyed. Perhaps Twyne's antiquarian interests made him protest too loudly at such destruction. It was when released from the Tower that he was sheltered in London by the printer Wolfe before he returned home. Back at Canterbury, Twyne was at once re-elected to Parliament, and became the city's mayor.

In Mary's reign, at the time of Wyatt's rebellion (a protest against Mary's plan to marry Philip II of Spain) Twyne raised 'an hundred honestest men of the town, being horsemen' to help pacify the country between London and Tonbridge where every town was said to be 'upp to drive away the Spaniards'. His contemporaries must have seen this incident as particularly significant for, apart from his headmastership, the fact that he was mayor during Wyatt's rebellion is the only event of his life mentioned on his memorial. Twyne was by then, it seems, firmly in sympathy with the Catholic party.

Early in 1561 Twyne was involved in a series of incidents which led a certain Joanna Basden (perhaps the mother of a scholar, William Basden) to take him to the Ecclesiastical Court of Canterbury, where she accused him of being 'a very conjurer'. Her story centred on her refusal to pay Twyne for improvements he had made to a house of hers which he was occupying. He was also offended, she claimed, because she had not made him an executor of her will.

At first he called her to his house, kept her waiting an hour and a half at the door and would then only let her in if she would say 'God save all' – thus asking for salvation for persons of all religious beliefs. This terrified Mrs Basden, who remembered that she had heard one of Twyne's students say that 'in wynter mornynges about v of clock whenas the scolers were come downe and had a good fyer to warme them, sodenly appeared a black thing likee a great rugged black dogg which wold daunce about the house and hurle fyer about the house'.

On another occasion Twyne called on Mrs Basden and 'by his couniuracion' made her house shake so violently that she thought it would collapse and was ill for three months from the shock.

Finally, Twyne arranged to meet her in the cathedral yard to discuss their disagreement. They argued for an hour and a half, during which Twyne used 'filthy

Above: Thomas Cranmer, the Archbishop whose ideas greatly influenced the establishment of the King's Scholars, painted at the age of 57 in 1546 by Gerlach Flicke.

Right: Matthew Parker, Archbishop under Elizabeth I, established scholarships for the School at Cambridge and planned a link for it with All Souls College at Oxford. He is painted here in his 70th year, encircled by his motto (I John 2, 17), by an unknown artist.

and unseemly talk', before, in exasperation, he started to shout at her 'get the out, get the out'. He then put a spell on her which prevented her moving and 'hurled stones at her so vehemently as the stones flying against the stone wall sprange out fyer', while he shouted at her, 'Away thou arraunt whoore, for I shall kill the . . .'. Here, unfortunately, the record of the case ends.

By this time Twyne had other troubles. In 1560 Queen Elizabeth's Archbishop Parker, on his first Visitation to Canterbury, required him 'to abstain from ryot and drunkeness, and not to intermeddle with any public office in the town'. It has generally been assumed that Parker's hostility to Twyne was a consequence of Twyne's Catholic sympathies. There could be another explanation. For a number of years Parker had been trying to recover Archbishop Cranmer's 'written books'. He may have disliked Twyne as a rival manuscript collector – which Twyne was. He may also have disliked him for his connection with the printer Wolfe, who had sheltered Twyne in London in Edward VI's reign. In 1563 Parker discovered that Wolfe's son-in-law, Stephen Nevinson, was in possession of some of Cranmer's books. Nevinson and Twyne may already have known each other. Certainly Nevinson was to write to William Cecil in 1573 to ask him to use his influence to have Twyne reinstated as headmaster because he had been improperly dismissed. Nevinson's letter is firm evidence that in about 1560 Parker did indeed dismiss Twyne, who did not resign. And Nevinson had first been supported at Cambridge by the Canterbury Dean and Chapter, then in 1560 become rector of Saltwood, Kent, and two years later a Canon of Canterbury. Though Parker in these years had been using Nevinson, he may already have suspected him, and this could have affected his attitude to Twyne.

Twyne's troubles continued. In 1562 he was again commanded to appear before the Privy Council, on what was probably some kind of a religious charge. And Archbishop Parker further persecuted him by depriving him of the keepership of some woods at Littlebourne. But at Canterbury he was never disgraced, and continued to be used by the Dean and Chapter as an occasional financial adviser.

Among his contemporaries it was not on his teaching or his political activities that his reputation was based, but on his learning. William Camden, author of *Britannia*, admired him, Holinshed, author of the *Chronicles*, wrote that he was 'a learned antiquarie, and no less furnished with old and autentyke monuments than ripe judgement and skillfull knowledge . . .'; and John Leland, Henry VIII's antiquarian, wrote a poem in his honour.

Various of Twyne's descendants became King's Scholars, then men of distinction, though at least two of them acquired the reputation Twyne acquired of dabbling in magic. His son, Thomas, a successful physician at Lewes, Sussex, was 'famed not only for medicine, but Astrology, and much respected by Dee and Allan' – two of the best known astrologers of Elizabethan times. It was Thomas Twyne who eventually published headmaster Twyne's *De Rebus Albionicis*.

Thomas's son, Brian, a learned antiquarian of the next century, took part in one of the great controversies of the time: was Oxford or Cambridge the older university? Anthony Wood gives him a long entry, no doubt because Wood so much regretted that a copy of Brian Twyne's book on Oxford which he had subsequently filled with annotations, was lost in a fire, forcing Wood to do much of his work again. About Brian Twyne, Wood writes that he was 'a severe Student and an adorer of venerable Antiquity', but admits that 'he was evilly spoken of by the *Oxonian* vulgar, as a conjurer, or one busied in the Black Art'.

The school of which Twyne was the master for so many years had almost certainly moved to the position given it by Anthony Wood – within the cemetery – before the Reformation. Wood perhaps copied William Somner who wrote in 1640, 'within the cemetery gate . . . I find yet standing the old School-house, now put to other use . . . . There are some that remember the Free School kept there, and that by one Mr Twyne . . .. For it was a Free School for the city chiefly, and so called, and sometime was of the liberty thereof . . . it was a place of situation, for privacy and retirement well chosen.'

The building is clearly shown on an Elizabethan map of the city (see *Plate 3*), standing due south of the cathedral, and there it still stands. Since Twyne's time it has indeed been put to other uses. In the eighteenth century bells were sometimes cast there, including 'Dunstan', the clock bell for the Cathedral's Oxford tower. It then became the cathedral's plumbery. In 1908 Woodruff and Cape describe it as 'a long narrow building, with walls of flint and a high-pitched tiled roof . . . now used as a stable and coach-house'. Today it is a public lavatory.

3

REFORM TRIUMPHANT

AFTER ITS REFOUNDING IN 1541 THE SCHOOL CONTINUED TO OCCUPY THE SCHOOLHOUSE SOUTH OF THE CATHEDRAL NEAR THE CEMETERY GATE FOR ANOTHER 17 YEARS before it was offered new premises. By then the old almonry buildings, on the opposite side of the cathedral at the north-west corner of the Precincts, had changed hands three times. At the Dissolution they had passed from the dissolved priory to the Dean and Chapter. In 1546 Dean Nicholas Wotton had obliged Henry VIII by handing them to the Crown as part of a complex exchange of properties and obligations. Eleven years later, Queen Mary, during her brief reign had given them 'at fee' (in perpetual leasehold) to her Cardinal Pole. Pole intended, according to his executor Aloysius Priuli, a Venetian aristocrat, to transfer them back to the Dean and Chapter for a school. It seems likely that he and the queen were planning a new cathedral school, to educate boys in the old faith. If so it is ironic that, after both of them had died within 12 hours of each other, Priuli should have carried out the letter of their intention for the benefit of the Protestant King's School. The Foundation (in practice the school) was granted the almonry site and buildings on a 500-year full-repairing lease at the annual rent of one peppercorn. The rent payments subsequently lapsed and when, in the 1930s, the school took advice it was told that Priuli's heirs were unlikely ever to be able to reclaim the Mint Yard.

For some reason in 1559, the year of the bequest, the almonry buildings themselves were not at once available, but the school nevertheless moved to the Mint Yard where instead it occupied the old North Hall. This great Norman building (154 feet long, 42 feet wide) had been substantially completed by 1165 and subsequently used by the monks as a hostel for poor pilgrims. Today its only surviving parts are the arches which supported it and the Norman staircase by which the scholars climbed to their new classroom.

When the school moved the Dean and Chapter spent £42 on converting the North Hall, but the building remained uncomfortable and Archbishop Parker, on the same visitation during which he ordered Twyne to behave soberly, told the dean to have the hall wainscotted and seats provided for the scholars. It was still unsatisfactory, and Dean William Godwin went to London to ask the queen if the school might move from the Mint Yard, where it was troubled by the fumes from the mint, to 'some other place within the syte of the Church'. But it was across the Mint Yard to the Almonry that, in 1573, the school moved, and there it stayed for the next 286 years.

Over this period its new premises grew dilapidated – in 1908 Woodruff and Cape wrote 'our fathers remember the ramshackle old buildings which for so many generations were dignified by the name of the King's School' – until, in 1865, plans for restoring them were abandoned and they were demolished. Even in 1573 they were old; the Almonry Chapel had been built in 1326. But in the 1570s an attempt was made at least to furnish them. A joiner, Mr More, was paid £5 for 20 'bedsteds in ye Mynt for ye scholers' – a number which might suggest that there were only 20 boarders among the 50 scholars, if we did not know of the three-to-a-bed sleeping arrangements for scholars at Wells.

Archbishop Parker continued to take a detailed interest in the school. On his second visitation he asked to be assured that the scholars were being taught from the Latin grammar approved by the queen. The book he referred to is generally known as *King Edward VIth's Latin Grammar* and it alone was officially approved in the province of Canterbury. And in 1574, the year before he died, he ordered a reform in the school's teaching methods, intended to connect it more closely with the cathedral's prebendaries and preachers. Each boy was to have one of these or the dean himself as his personal tutor. The dean told Parker that these learned men were often away from Canterbury and too busy to act as tutors.

Parker also, at his own expense, created university scholarships for King's Scholars, so putting right one of the unfortunate consequences of the 1546 deal between Dean Wotton and Henry VIII. By this Henry, in return for the Almonry site and other properties had not only given the Dean and Chapter the manor of Godmersham, but had relieved them of the obligation laid on them by the 1541 Statutes to contribute £200 a year to support 24 scholars at the universities. Since the 1546 agreement there had been no university scholarships for the school, and Dean Wotton had personally, for example, to support at Oxford the young man who was to succeed Twyne as headmaster: Anthony Rushe. Parker now settled on the Cambridge college of Corpus Christi, where he had been the master until he became archbishop, certain Westminster properties which would enable it to provide three scholars from the King's School with 'convenient and free chamber or chambers, Commons, Barber, Launder, Beddings and other necessities'. The Parker scholarships still continue, and have been held by many notable King's Scholars, Christopher Marlowe among them.

If Parker had lived longer he might have connected the school with an Oxford college as closely as Winchester became connected with New College or Eton with King's. In 1571, the year in which the King's Scholar Richard Hovenden became Warden of All Souls, Hovenden recorded that buildings were being converted for such scholars. The following year the project was interrupted by the Plague and by the time Parker died in 1575 it had not been revived.

Anthony Rushe was not only Dean Wotton's protégé but a man well suited to be the new headmaster. In his letter recommending Rushe to Archbishop Parker, Wotton describes him as sober, honest and hard working. 'For his learninge,' Wotton writes, 'he is lyke to satisfye ye roome very well.' Wotton did not add, though he must have known, that Rushe, during his years at Magdalen College, had shown himself suitable in another way. In Mary's reign, when Mass was again being celebrated in the college chapel, he had refused to attend, and been punished by the vice-president.

During Rushe's time the scholars were still fed at the Common Table with the junior members of the cathedral establishment, and an account book of 1562–3 shows exactly what they ate. In the week before Christmas on a typical day, dinner was milk and beef, and supper soup of lamb's neck and breast. Butter, whiting, dab, and eggs are the only other items listed until Christmas Day itself when the joint was leg of lamb, and flour, raisins, prunes, cloves, mace, and pepper, which were presumably made into a somewhat sour Christmas pudding. Bread and beer for the week are listed and costed separately. On Friday there was an issue of brown salt and mustard, but not a single vegetable is mentioned.

In a Lent week by contrast no meat was served. On a typical day there was milk, butter, and salt fish for dinner and red herring for supper. On two days there was only one meal. And though there were sometimes 'pese', no bread or beer are listed. The full cost of food for the week in Lent was less than half that for the week before Christmas. Although it was over 20 years since the Reformation and four since Mary had died, the old fasting rules for Lent were still being observed.

At about the same time (1562–3) the Dean and Chapter gave Rushe £3 *6s 8d* towards the 'settynge out of his plays at Christmass'. Both previous histories of the school misread the sum as £14 *6s 8d*, and speculated that such a large amount might have been for a stage. The correct sum is in line with Rushe's next recorded grant of *56s 8d*, for 'settyng further Tragedies, Comedys, and interludes this next Christmas'. School plays were a fashion of the period – at Eton some 30 years earlier the headmaster, Nicholas Udall, had written the first English comedy, *Ralph Roister Doister*, and Christmas plays at Canterbury became a tradition.

There was one unstaged dramatic incident during Rushe's five years as headmaster, when Dr Bullen, one of the cathedral prebendaries threatened to strike Rushe. But Rushe seems only to have accidentally become involved in this feud between Bullen and the dean, whom Bullen said he would nail to the wall with his sword.

Rushe, according to Anthony Wood's *Athenae Oxonienses*, was a 'florid and frequent' preacher. His sermons were admired by Queen Elizabeth, and within a year of his leaving the school in 1565 he became a canon at Windsor. His book, *A President for a Prince*, he dedicated to the queen, and he might have risen high in the Church if he had not died at the age of 40.

During the next 25 years Rushe was followed in fairly quick succession by five headmasters, about only one of whom is much known. He was John Gresshop, who came from Christ Church, Oxford, and stayed longest, holding the position from 1566 till his death early in 1580. He was unmarried, and apparently had no relatives at Canterbury, because various members of the cathedral foundation compiled an inventory of his possessions, and it is this which shows what Gresshop must have looked like and what sort of man he was.

Among his clothes were two pairs of hose, two old doublets, a Spanish leather jerkin, a cap, and a hat. Also a cassock, some old gowns, and old cloaks. One of the doublets and one pair of hose were of 'rash' (smooth silk or worsted) and no doubt these formed his best suit, but the only garment of style was a damask jacket with a silk girdle, dating perhaps from his Oxford days. To his pupils he must have appeared comfortably shabby.

His books are even more revealing. In 'the upper study by the schoole door' there were 217 volumes and in the 'lower study' another 125. He thus had, in the words of William Urry, 'a larger private library than almost anyone outside of the circles of bishops and noblemen, far greater than the private collections of university dons'. The inventory gives a full list of Gresshop's books; many were Latin and Greek classics, but there was also much Reformation literature (by Luther, John Knox, and Thomas More, for example), several Bibles in Latin, Greek, and English, various books of English poetry including a copy of Chaucer, and some medical books, gruesomely illustrated with diagrams of dissections and surgeon's tools.

Besides clothes, books, a number of 'coarse sheets for boys', and such curious domestic items as pewter chamber pots and a silver whistle (for controlling his pupils?), Gresshop left debts to at least fifteen tradesmen, which provide further evidence that he was housing boarders. These were duly settled a few months later, and among those who got his money (16*s* 4*d*) was John Marlowe. Marlowe was a Canterbury shoemaker, and, for the last 12 months before Gresshop died, his son Christoper Marlowe had been one of Gresshop's scholars.

Is this Christopher Marlowe? The young man's age is right (21) and the painting was found at Corpus Christi, Marlowe's college at Cambridge. It is hard, though scholarly, to resist the splendid brow, the bold eye and the flaunt of finery above Marlowe's proper social station.

Christopher Marlowe could well be described as the King's School's most famous scholar. Unfortunately, more is known about his father's Canterbury affairs than about Christopher's. John Marlowe had started his shoe shop in 1564 or 1565 and subsequently employed a total of five apprentices as well as several occasional servants. But he was a bad manager of money, regularly failing to pay his rates, rent, and other debts. Two of his landlords brought court actions against him. As Churchwarden of St Mary Breadman he was accused by his fellow churchwardens of failing to pay the clerk's wages. And when, in 1589, he was (surprisingly) elected Warden and Treasurer of the Shoemakers' Company he failed at the end of the year to produce the company's credit balance of 40*s* 10*d*, with the result that the company also took him to law. Marlowe claimed that he had handed over the sum, but the jury found against him.

These are only a small sample of John Marlowe's usually discreditable financial and legal entanglements. The picture they give of a man with continual money troubles creates a mystery. When his son, Christopher, became a King's Scholar at Christmas 1578 he was already 14 years and 10 months old. He must have had some previous education, either private or at a school, possibly even as a commoner at the King's School, but it seems improbable that his father could have paid for this. Christopher may have had a Canterbury patron, but there is no firm evidence that he was Sir Roger Manwood, a local judge, as sometimes suggested on the grounds that Marlowe must have written his very distinctive epitaph in St Stephen's Church.

Marlowe was a King's Scholar for about 21 months, and though nothing is known about him while he was at the school, the fact that for 12 of these months the learned Mr Gresshop was his master is, to say the least, suggestive. Not only

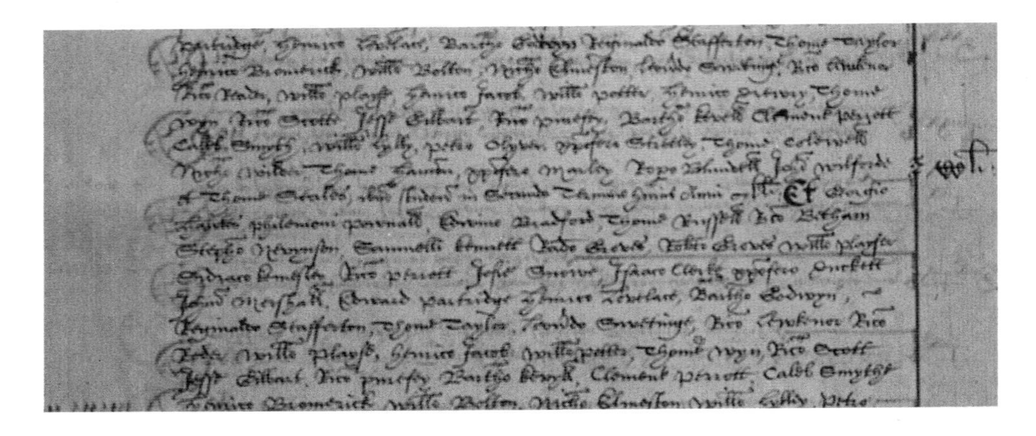

The Cathedral Treasurer's accounts for 1578/79 show that he handed to Christopher Marlowe – 'Chr'ofero Marley' – his King's Scholarship money. Henry Jacob's name appears three lines earlier.

was one part of Gresshop's library shelved 'in the upper study by the schoole door', so presumably available to the boys, but a number of the books it contained appear to have influenced Marlowe's writing – Fenton's *Discourse of the Warres in France* to name just one.

The lower master throughout Marlowe's time at the school, Robert Rose, may also have been important to him. Rose had been a King's Scholar himself before going to St John's College, Cambridge. He was lower master for 14 years, and remained keenly interested in the school. In 1618, 33 years after he had left it, he gave land to support four university exhibitions for King's Scholars.

A less exemplary character whom Marlowe would certainly have known was James Felle, who came from Bolton, Lancashire, and was the school's cook. Cooking does not seem to have taken all Felle's time, for he was able to moonlight as a court attendant, gaoler, cathedral rent-collector, and escort for prisoners on their way to the Privy Council. In the year Marlowe left the school, Felle was charged with stealing a ring from the purse of Esther Kemp, a woman of ill repute – though this does not necessarily imply a relationship with Esther, but may have been an episode in a quarrel between Esther and Felle's wife.

Boys are as likely to be influenced by their fellow students as by their masters. In total Marlowe's scholar contemporaries numbered about 80, few enough for him to have known them all. The later lives of the great majority were conventional. Either they became Anglican clergymen or retired to their native parts of Kent to live as yeomen and country gentlemen. Two became lawyers, and four teachers of various sorts. But one or two had dramatic careers, and may well have stood out as schoolboys.

Henry Jacob, a slightly junior contemporary of Marlowe's, who left the school in 1581, was forced to escape abroad because of his puritan nonconformity. He spent various periods in the Netherlands, associating there with fellow puritans who later became known as the Pilgrim Fathers group. Back in England, he established the country's first Congregationalist Church, then in Virginia founded the settlement named after him: Jacobopolis.

It was no doubt because Samuel Kennett – who probably arrived at the school a few months before Marlowe – was also known as 'a most terrible puritan' that on leaving he became warder at the Tower of London, in charge of Roman

Thomas Wilson, Lower Master in 1586. Was he ahead of his time when he wrote that 'it is necessary in Grammar Schools, that children which learn French, Latine, or Greek, have their Dictionaries & Lexicons allowed them'?

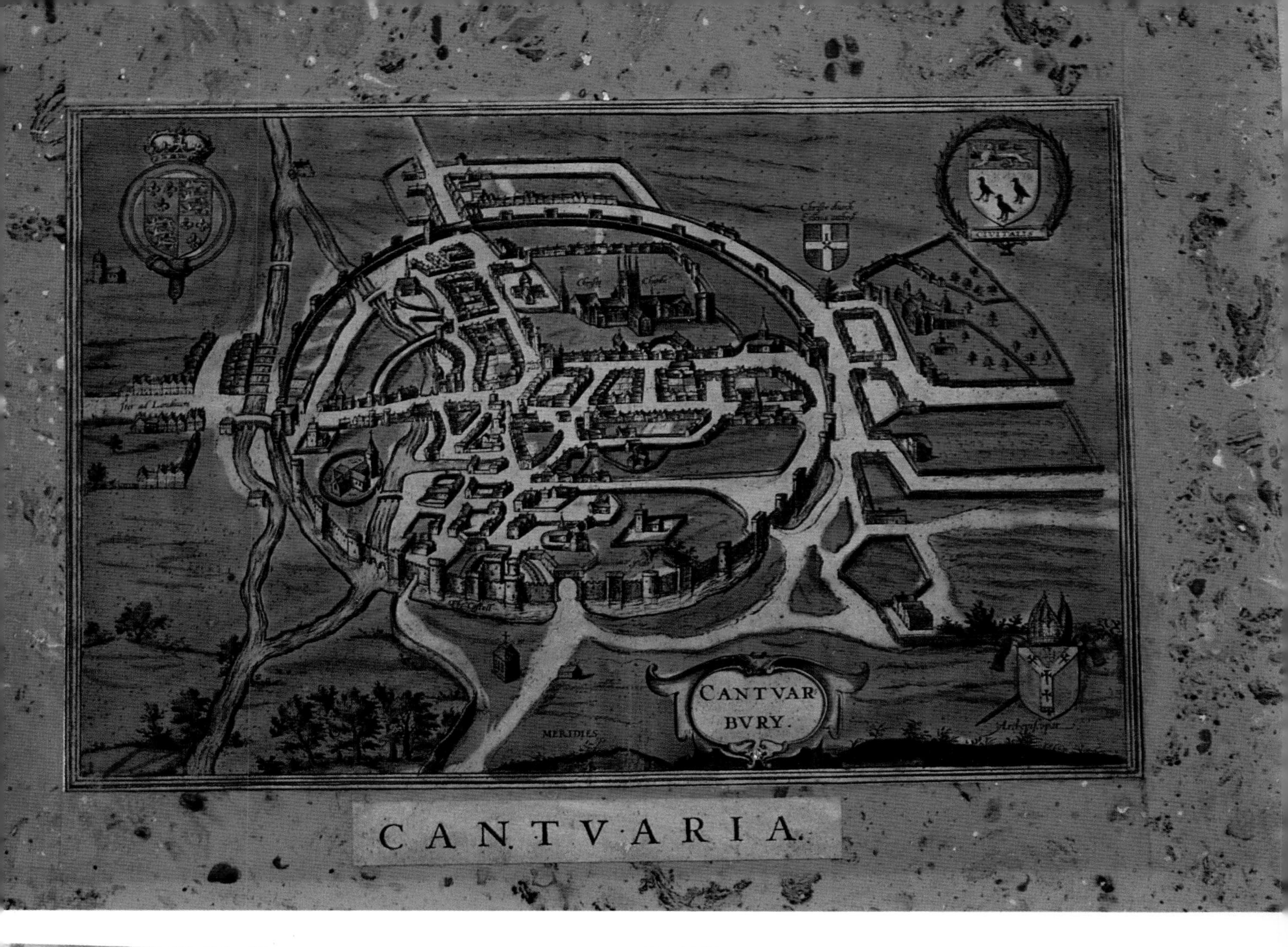

PLATE 3

Above: Canterbury under Elizabeth I. The old Schoolhouse with its garden is clearly marked South of the Cathedral.

Left: Mid-seventeenth century Canterbury. School buildings from Blackfriars to St. Augustine's with its elaborate knot-gardens are all noted.

PLATE 4

Cardinal Pole, after Sebastiano del Piombo. In 1559 the Cardinal bequeathed the Mint Yard and its Almonry for the School's use.

A fore-edge painting of the Almonry Chapel and the Green Court Gate in abo 1820. The Almonry was the chief School building from Elizabeth I to Victoria

Catholic prisoners. But one of the prisoners, a priest named John Hart, had his revenge, converting Kennett to Catholicism, thus forcing him to flee abroad. After a period at Rheims, Kennett went to Rome and himself became a priest, then returned to England under the assumed name of William Carter. Here he was probably an underground priest or spy. Abroad again at the start of James I's reign, he became a Benedictine monk, then returned once more to England as part of the mission to the north.

Kennett was by no means the only King's Scholar to become an active member of the Roman Catholic opposition to Queen Elizabeth. In 1586 Thomas Bramston, a seminary priest, who had been 'brought up in the Grammar School at Canterbury under old Mr Twyne' was examined by the Privy Council. Thomas Stapleton, described by Wood as 'the most learned Roman Catholic of all his time', was also taught by Twyne until the age of twelve. Under Mary he became a Canon of Chichester, but when Elizabeth succeeded he emigrated to Louvain. Here he made a translation of Bede's *Ecclesiastical History*, dedicating it to the queen, so that she would understand 'the ancient Faith and Religion of our Ancestors'. Subsequently he wrote many theological works and became famous among European Catholics. Friends were surprised that he was never made a cardinal and though he received offers from the Pope of positions at Rome he returned to Louvain where he died in 1598.

William Weston, a scholar in the 1560s under Rushe, while at Oxford came under the influence of Edmund Campion, and after leaving spent 20 years abroad, becoming a priest at Cordoba. In 1584 he returned as Superior of a Jesuit mission, and for the next two years travelled the country, sometimes taking the name of Edmonds after Campion, making converts who included the Earl of Arundel and casting out devils. 'Eyewitnesses . . . actually saw the devils gliding about in immense numbers under the skins of the possessed like fishes swimming.' But in 1586 he was arrested and held in prison for the rest of Elizabeth's reign. Abroad again, he ultimately became Rector of the English College at Valladolid.

The fact that men of this sort had been educated at the King's School would have been known to Catholics abroad, and must have made it easier for Marlowe to play the part he was almost certainly to play, of another Catholic defector.

The date when Marlowe left the King's School is known from the buttery books and college records of Corpus Christi College, Cambridge. Here, at the buttery he paid 1*d* on about 10 December 1580. The following week he paid it the large sum of 3*s* 1½*d*. In March 1581 he officially matriculated, and from this time received regular quarterly sums of 12 or 13 shillings as a Parker Scholar.

During the next six years there is only one interesting feature of Marlowe's financial records: reduced income payments and an absence of buttery entries on an increasing number of occasions show that he was absent for parts of certain terms. These absences are almost certainly explained by what happened in 1587 when the university would not grant him his MA degree. Remarkably, Marlowe then obtained the support of the Privy Council, which told the university that 'Christopher Morley' had 'done Her Majesty good service' and 'it was not Her Majesty's pleasure that anyone employed as he had been in matters touching the benefit of his country should be defamed by those that are ignorant of the affairs

William Weston SJ, King's Scholar 1562–65, courageous and scholarly but also with 'singular dominion over devils' : a man of his watershed time.

he went about'. Rumours that he planned to settle at Rheims, the Privy Council wrote, 'should be allayed by all possible means'. Rheims was a gathering place for plotting Catholics. The implication is clear: Marlowe had been making visits to Rheims, and the university, not understanding why, had decided that he was politically dangerous. The Privy Council knew the truth: that Marlowe had been there as an English spy.

From the time he left Cambridge, five strands can be seen in Marlowe's life. Firstly, he wrote the well-known plays. Even these are surrounded by mystery. We do not know when or in what order he wrote them. He may indeed have written some at Cambridge. Nor do we know how much of the surviving texts are really his, where they were performed, or what his audiences thought of them.

Secondly, he continued to be involved in 'matters touching the benefit of his country', as well as in less approved matters like coining in Holland. For obvious reasons the exact nature of what he was doing is even harder to discover.

Thirdly and more publicly, he was no less than four times involved in affrays which brought him into contact with the law, one of them at Canterbury. Who is to say how many quarrels or fights remain unrecorded?

Fourthly, he had a relationship, probably homosexual, with Thomas Walsingham, owner of the thousand-acre estate of Scadbury at Chislehurst, cousin of Francis Walsingham, Queen Elizabeth's spymaster (a connection conceivably first arranged by the King's Scholar, Nicholas Faunt, who left Corpus Christi just before Marlowe arrived there and became Francis's trusted secretary/spy).

Fifthly, Marlowe moved increasingly among people known for their atheistic views. It was because he was suspected of these that he was eventually, in May 1593, called before the Privy Council, where his accuser, Baines, also claimed that Marlowe had said, 'all they that love not tobacco and boys were fools'.

He was at liberty on bail on 30 May that year, and on that day he was killed at Deptford. Because of his spying activities, because he was under government suspicion, and because the three men with him at the time are known to have been agents, it is often claimed that Marlowe was murdered. To make the setting fit the crime, the place where he died is said to have been a tavern or a brothel. In fact, as William Urry shows, the place was a respectable lodging house, kept by one Mrs Eleanor Bull, a woman of good family. But about Marlowe's death, Urry accepts the more prosaic verdict of the coroner's jury, that it was the result of a quarrel between the four men about who should pay for supper that evening. This version describes in detail the positions of the four men in the room, the way in which Marlowe attacked one of them, Ingram Frizer, and how Frizer, trapped at the table and wounded, defended himself by grabbing Marlowe's weapon and killing him by striking him above the eye.

In 1956 a well-argued case against this version of events was published by Calvin Hoffman in his *The Man who was Shakespeare*. There are reasons, Hoffman points out, for seeing the coroner's report as hastily contrived and specifically designed to show that Frizer could be exonerated for acting in self-defence. It is also full of improbabilities. And there are reasons for thinking that the whole affair was plotted by Thomas Walsingham. Frizer had regularly worked for Walsingham, and returned to him the day after his pardon and release. Another of the three, Robert Poley, came to Deptford from Holland, visiting just one person on the way: Thomas Walsingham at Scadbury Park. Walsingham may well have wanted Marlowe out of the way for fear of what he would tell the Privy Council.

Hoffman, however, went on to claim that a substitute vagrant was murdered and Marlowe was spirited away to Italy where he wrote the works of William Shakespeare – a theory which must unfortunately be placed in the ley-line, flying-saucer class. His obsessive interest in Marlowe led to Hoffman endowing a valuable literary prize for Marlowe studies (worth £7100 in 1990), which the King's School administers.

Two headmasters about whom little is known followed Gresshop, then came Anthony Shorte, who was not a success. His health was poor, for in 1584 the Dean and Chapter granted him five marks (£3 *6s 8d*) 'to encourage hym in his diligence and paynestakinge in teachinge, and for the Reliefe of his charges in his late sykness'. Four years later they ordered him 'to have a greter care, and to be more diligent than he hath byn that the scholars of the schole may better profit in learning, as well as in good manners and civility, than late they have done'. Shorte complied and in 1590 they gave him a reward of £2 13*s* 4*d*, but the next year he died, leaving a widow and six children in 'distressed case'. As she had inherited nothing from Shorte, the Dean and Chapter awarded her a pension of £6 13*s* 4*d* a year.

Failure Shorte may have been, but he helped to educate a boy even more distinguished in his field than Marlowe, about whom more is known: William Harvey. Harvey arrived at the school in 1588, at the age of ten, but as his name does not appear on the 1588 or 1590 lists of scholars – the only ones surviving for his years – he was probably a commoner. His family home was at Folkestone so he may have been a boarder. On the other hand, he had three maternal uncles named Halke living at Canterbury and he perhaps lodged with one of them. At this time there was an apothecary named Richard Halke at Canterbury who was probably one of these uncles. Perhaps Harvey lodged with, or at least knew, this apothecary uncle and first became interested in medicine in his shop.

John Aubrey's brief life of Harvey is one of his most entertaining, and to be trusted since he and Harvey became good friends. Harvey's education at the King's School, and later at Caius College, Cambridge, apparently left him with disadvantages. 'He wrote a very bad hand,' Aubrey says, and 'very bad Latin'. His famous *Circulation of the Blood* had to be translated into Latin for him. On the other hand, he could understand Greek and Latin, and would tell Aubrey to 'goe to the Fountain head, and read Aristotle, Cicero, Avicenna, and did call the Neoteriques shitt-breeches'. Surprisingly, Harvey 'did not care for chymistrey'. His bills (prescriptions) were considered worthless by fellow doctors. It is tempting to suggest that some of Harvey's other habits and opinions were formed at school, for example a habit of sitting and meditating for two or three hours at a time in one of the caves he had dug for him around his house at Combe, Surrey; and his opinion that 'man was but a great mischievous Baboon'.

To succeed Shorte, the Dean and Chapter chose an experienced teacher, Roger Raven, an old King's Scholar. Archbishop Whitgift, recommending Raven to the dean, wrote that he had had 'some long continuance and practise in keepinge a scholle at Wrotham in Kent'. The choice seems to have been a satisfactory one. Raven was headmaster for 24 years, and by the end of his time the school is said to have had a total of 200 pupils. While he was headmaster James I survived the Gunpowder Plot, and from 1613 onwards the school celebrated his escape with bonfires, plays, and speeches. That year, to encourage these loyal festivities, the Dean and Chapter granted it six shillings.

William Harvey, discoverer of the circulation of the blood. Probably its most remarkable pupil, Harvey was a commoner throughout his time at the School (1588–93). This 1739 engraving by Jacob Houbraken is based on an earlier portrait.

4

MASTER LUDD THE SURVIVOR

WHEN ROGER RAVEN DIED IN 1615 HE WAS SUCCEEDED BY HIS OWN LOWER MASTER, JOHN LUDD. LUDD CAME FROM A HUMBLE FAMILY, BUT ONE WELL CONNECTED WITH Canterbury. His father had been a verger, and his maternal grandfather a cathedral carpenter. He himself had been a King's Scholar. At the same time that Ludd succeeded Raven, Raven's son succeeded Ludd as lower master, and these two ran the school for the next 18 years. Ludd continued to be headmaster for another 16 years, the last nine of which were years of revolution and civil war. Whatever else may be said of him, he was a survivor.

William Somner, compiler of the first Anglo-Saxon dictionary. Elected a King's Scholar in 1615, he so loved Canterbury that 'neither mind nor body could be mov'd to any distance from it'. (An engraving by M. Burghers, late 17th century.)

All went smoothly for 20 years, indeed in the 1620s and 30s the Dean and Chapter made the first recorded grants for school sporting events. These consisted of races, probably on foot, but perhaps on horseback, on Barham Down. On one occasion the races were to be run against other scholars (*contra alios scholares*) – who these scholars were is a mystery.

In 1635, however, William Laud, who had by then been Archbishop of Canterbury for two years, began to say severe things about the school. How was it, he wrote to the dean, that barely two boys could 'make and understand any ordinary Greek prose or verse, whereas twenty years before all the Upper Form could do so . . .? This must needs be the Master's fault, for the head form is not under the usher [lower master], and besides I hear many complaints against his negligence.'

Ludd replied that the Upper Form had never been more proficient in Greek. More than two of its members could speak the language, and not more than six had ever been able to. It was unfortunate that one of the best scholars had recently died of smallpox, which for the last two years had 'hindered' the school. (Epidemics were a recurring problem, and two years later the school was closed because of the Plague, to all students who 'lodged without the church'.) In further defence of his record, Ludd supplied the dean with a list of distinguished scholars – now lost but no doubt including many of the 37 MAs he would claim that he had educated.

William Somner was as learned as any of the 37 though he never went to a university. Somner had come to the King's School at the age of eight, in the same year that Ludd became headmaster and had subsequently worked at Canterbury where Archbishop Laud had promoted him to be Registrar of the Ecclesiastical

Courts. His support for Laud led to his being described by Puritans as 'one of Laud's creatures'. All his life he was a traditionalist. His hobby was shooting with the long bow, which, in the words of his biographer (Bishop White Kennett, 1693) 'no doubt he lov'd as much for the antiquity, as for the health and pleasure of that manly sport'.

But it was his Anglo-Saxon studies which made him a well-known scholar; eventually in 1659 he published an Anglo-Saxon dictionary. And his *Antiquities of Canterbury*, dedicated to Laud, remains a unique source of information about the city in his time. Fortunately, the book was published in 1640, and so records many features of the cathedral which were soon afterwards destroyed.

In practice as well as in print Somner preserved features of the old cathedral. When the Puritans wrecked its ornaments, statues, and glass, Somner 'diverted the thieves and concealed the treasure', giving some to people who would not be suspected and keeping some himself. 'When the beautiful Font . . . was pull'd down, and the materials carried away by the rabble, he enquir'd with great diligence for all the scatter'd pieces, bought them up at his own charge, kept them safe till the King's return, and then delivered them to that worthy Bishop [John Warner, Bishop of Rochester, the original donor]; who reedified his Font, and made it a greater beauty of holyness; giving Mr Somner the just honour, to have a daughter of his own first baptised in it.' Somner also planned a book on the antiquities of Kent, but the only part published was a study of Roman ports and forts, and unfortunately most of his papers were destroyed soon after his death by a fire in the audit-house. Towards the end of the Commonwealth (1659) he spent time in prison at Deal Castle for trying 'to get hands to petition for a Free Parliament'.

All his life Somner remained keenly interested in his old school. 'He was frequently entrusted by the Dean and Prebendaries, to supervise the public School, to examine Lads, that should be elected King's Scholars; and . . . to judge who were most fit for removal to the Universities . . . . His endeavours were to advance the interest and honour of the School, to as high a pitch, as while he was himself a member of it.'

The dean also wrote to Archbishop Laud to defend Ludd's teaching, adding that Ludd had never made the parents or governors of his pupils pay more than they wished to pay. But Laud maintained what seems to have been a campaign against the headmaster for his slack management of the school. In 1637 the archbishop obtained the King's approval of revised Statutes for the cathedral which gave fresh instructions for the running of the school.

There were to be school monitors 'to keep an eye on the behaviour of the other boys as well in church as in School and elsewhere lest anything unseemly or disgraceful be done'. Monitors who misbehaved were to be flogged as an example to the rest. The fact that monitors were now ordered suggests that this was their beginning.

The arrangements for examining boys were to be consolidated into a great annual examination of every boy by the headmaster, dean, and canons in residence, who would send a written report to the archbishop. This would include comments on the keenness or slackness of masters.

The scholars were to attend cathedral services even more often than before, on the vigils of feasts as well as on actual feast days. About this time a visiting lieutenant from Norwich saw them there and described them in their white surplices as 'a snowy crowd of King's Scholars, which were fifty in number'. And daily morning prayers were now to be held in 'some chapel or other place in the Church' rather than in the school. The place chosen was the Chapter House, also called the Sermon House, and here the boys were disciplined by a kind of janitor who was paid five shillings a quarter to 'keep them in good order, and prevent others going upp into the gallery'. Soon after the Restoration one Thomas Flood, who had had this job, petitioned the dean for 30 shillings back pay.

William Laud took a close interest in the School and made substantial changes in the Statutes relating to it. (An engraving by D. Loggan, 17th century, after van Dyck.)

The revised Statutes also attempted to revive the Common Table, probably abandoned by 1624 at the latest, but added 'if the Dean and Chapter could conveniently arrange that this should be done'. There is no evidence that they ever did.

There were dramatic events at Canterbury in the 1640s and 50s, in which a number of King's Scholars besides Somner were involved, by no means all of them Royalists. The background to these was that the elderly Dean Isaac Bargrave (a King's Scholar in 1592) and the cathedral establishment were sympathetic to the King while the mayor and city corporation favoured Parliament. Early in 1642 Bargrave created a store of arms and ammunition in the deanery and cathedral, thinking perhaps that the walled Precincts could become a Royalist fort. It was to search for these that Colonel Edwin Sandys (perhaps on home ground – several Edwin Sandyses occur in King's School lists) arrived in August the same year with a company of Parliamentary troopers. The dean was away but they pulled Mrs Bargrave out of bed, and took away his son together with two cartloads of arms and six barrels of powder. At the same time the troopers carried out the sacking of the cathedral already mentioned.

Another old King's Scholar, the notorious Revd Richard Culmer, in his pamphlet *Cathedrall Newes from Canterbury*, gives a vivid account of this sacking. 'Some zealous Troopers,' he writes, '. . . fought . . . with the Cathedral Gods . . . namely, Altars, Images, Service-booke, Prickesong-booke, Surplisse, and Organs; for they hewed the Altar-railes all to pieces, and threw their Altar over, and over, and over, downe the three Altar-steps, and left it lying with the heeles upward; they slasht some Images, Crucifixes, and Pricksong bookes and one greasie Service-booke, and a ragged smock of the whore of Rome, called a Surplisse, and began to play the tune of the zealous souldier, on the Organs, or case of whistles which never were in tune since . . . .'

Culmer had been at the King's School during Raven's time, when, his son claims, he was 'senier of all that school' (though his name does not come especially high in the school lists, which usually indicate seniority), then at Magdalene College, Cambridge, where, according to hostile pamphlets, he was 'famous . . . for foot-ball playing and swearing, but never thought to be cut out for a Mercury' (a hawker of pamphlets etc. – *O.E.D.*). The same pamphlets accuse him of pulling out the spigots of the wine barrels in his college cellar. Soon afterwards he became a zealous Puritan. His first living was at Goodnestone, Kent, and it was here, when he refused to read 'the King's Book of Sabbath recreations' that Archbishop Laud suspended him and he and the archbishop became violent enemies. Out of work for three years and seven months, Culmer claimed that he was destitute, and had seven children to support, so small that he could and did carry them all at once on his back. At this time he was sent briefly to the Fleet Prison for bringing a false and malicious accusation against one of his enemies.

By August 1642 he was living at Canterbury, but took no part in Colonel Sandys's destruction of the twenty-sixth. It must have left him dissatisfied because, on 13 December the following year, when he had been made one of the ministers responsible for detecting and demolishing superstitious inscriptions and idolatrous monuments, he and his fellow commissioners returned to the cathedral.

'When the commissioners entered ... that Cathedrall,' he writes, 'they knew not where to begin, the Images and Pictures were so numerous, as if that Superstitious Cathedrall had been built for no other end but to be a stable for Idolls. At last they resolved to begin with the window on the East of the high Altar, beyond that Sainted-Traytor, Arch-Bishop Beckets shrine ....' Presently Culmer himself went to work, using as his guide William Somner's recently published book. 'This booke was a card and compasse to sail by, in that Cathedrall Ocean of Images: by it many a Popish picture was discovered and demolished ... here is the wonder, that this booke should be a means to pull down Idols, which so much advanceth Idolatry .... A minister [himself] being then on top of the citie ladder, near 60 steps high, with a whole pike in his hand ratling down proud Beckets glassy bones

'Ratling down proud Becket's glassy bones' in Canterbury Quire, supervised by Parliament's commissioners, seated in the centre of the Quire, hats firmly on. (Oil by Thomas Johnson, 1657.)

*The detail (*below*) shows a man smashing a window in Canterbury Quire, on the right side of the picture.*

(others present, would not adventer so high) to him it was said 'tis a shame for a minister to be seen there; the Minister replyed, Sir I count it no shame, but an honour, my Mr. whipt the living buyers and sellers out of the Temple; these are dead Idylls.... Some wisht he might break his neck, others said it should cost bloud. But he finished the worke and came downe well, and was in very good health when this was written.'

Culmer had popular as well as municipal support in Canterbury, where many foreign Calvinists lived. In January 1642 during cathedral services there had been shouts from the congregation of 'This is idolatry' and 'Down with the Altar'. And that year the mayor and other citizens had published a declaration that 'the said Richard Culmer . . . was a man of exemplary life and conversation'. But some felt that he had gone too far. According to William Gostling (*A Walk in and about the city of Canterbury, 1777*), while Culmer 'was laying about him with all the zeal of a renegado, a townsman, who was among those who were looking at him, desired to know what he was doing. "I am doing the work of the Lord," says he; "then", replied the other "if it please the Lord, I will help you," and threw a stone with so good a will, that if the saint had not ducked, he might have laid his own bones among the rubbish he was making'. According to Culmer's son's defence of his father (*Parish Looking-Glasse*) Culmer's 'bloud was then threatened by some that stood without the iron gates, in the body of the Church: But Mr John Lade, Mayor of Canterbury, sent a file of Musqueteers, who conveyed M. Culmer safe home to his own house'.

The following year Culmer was appointed to the living of Minster in the Isle of Thanet (his family came from Thanet). Here his new parishioners, warned about his reputation, first locked him out of his own church so that he had to climb in by a broken window, then when they let him out, beat him until he was covered in blood. Eventually they offered to pay him the whole income of the living if he would go away so that they could choose someone else. Culmer refused. He much disliked black clothing, and it was because he would wear a blue gown that he became known as 'Blue Dick' or 'Blue-skin Dick of Thanet'. At the Restoration he was finally ejected and soon afterwards spent a second spell in prison, accused of plotting, though his guilt was not proved. Laud, before his execution, described Culmer as 'one of the most daring schismatics in all the country'.

Meanwhile, at Canterbury, Ludd himself had been in trouble. In 1645 and again in 1646 he was called before the Mayor of Canterbury and other officials of the county and city to answer 'scandalous charges'. Though Ludd survived, he was clearly a suspected Royalist who, in an unostentatious way, had continued to manage his school as he had been managing it for the previous 30 years. Like Twyne after the Reformation, Ludd had influencial friends in the city, particularly his brother Thomas Ludd, an alderman and a puritan, and perhaps they defended him.

The school had another supporter. By this time the revenues of the abolished Dean and Chapter had been put into the hands of a treasurer, Captain Thomas Monins. Monins, also a King's Scholar, did much during the next five years (1644–9) to keep his old school financed and its buildings intact. The salaries of the two masters (still £20 and £10 a year respectively) were paid and so were the allowances of the students (still £4 a year). Money was provided for the repair of the cathedral and of 'the several Houses and buildings within the Precincts'. In April 1649 Monins's account book records that 'the school had a great repair'. Even when he had left his job in 1649 and taken command of a troop of horse, Monins continued to be involved with Canterbury affairs, perhaps because he still occupied his commodious house on the south side of the churchyard with its gardens of fruit trees, stable, and large courtyard. When the water supply to various Precincts houses was cut off, it was Monins who asked Parliament what should be done.

After the Restoration, Monins petitioned Charles II that he might be restored to favour and keep his troop of horse, since he had 'preserved this Cathedral from ruin as well as the buildings and other matters belonging to it whilst he was Treasurer, and . . . having secreted the church Muniments and Plate . . . restored them at the Restoration'. But he was not forgiven.

As in any civil war, there were other King's Scholars besides Monins who had divided loyalties or vacillated, the best known Sir Edward Dering (K.S. 1603), who in 1640 was elected Member for Kent of what became the Long Parliament. Dering was a Kentish gentleman, connected by marriage to James I's boyfriend, the Duke of Buckingham, and in these years had clear Royalist sympathies. Early in Charles I's reign (1629) he was made Lieutenant of Dover Castle. But his views and whole life were altered when he and Archbishop Laud quarrelled over their rival parsons for Pluckley – a parish where the archbishop had the gift of the living, but the Dering family had so much power that they used the church as a barn. Dering, like Richard Culmer but for entirely different reasons, became a violent enemy of Laud's, and it was for this reason rather than as a Puritan that, the year after his election to Parliament, he introduced the Root and Branch Bill for the abolition of Bishops, Deans, and Chapters.

He soon discovered that his own intention, which was not to 'destroy the function of Episcopacy' but to 'un-Lord them from a domineering power', was being hijacked by puritan extremists, and by the time the war began had again become a Royalist; he raised a cavalry regiment to fight for the King.

The fact that, two years later, he was not one of the Royalists who followed Charles abroad but paid £1000 to make peace with Parliament, is less easily explained away. His *A Discourse on Sacrifice* (1644) suggests that his dislike of high church ritual had genuinely been rearoused. But the true reason is probably that by nature he was an antiquarian rather than a politician or soldier. While Lieutenant of Dover Castle he discovered there the Magna Carta now at the British Museum.

Unlike Dering, some King's Scholars took full advantage of Parliament's success. John Lee (K.S. 1622–4), Mayor of Canterbury in 1652, would have had the cathedral demolished (on Parliament's orders) if he could have found workmen willing to do it. On the other hand, George Mullins (K.S. 1615–17) was dismissed as an alderman after the Kentish rising of 1648; Edward Aldey (K.S. 1609–12), Vicar of St Andrew's, preached on Christmas Day, 1647, when the mayor had ordered that the shops should open and it should be treated like any other day; and John Boys (K.S. 1616–19) organized the 1659 petition for a freely elected Parliament, for the support of which William Somner was imprisoned.

A King's Scholar who was less involved in the religious controversies of the time was the plant collector, John Tradescant. His father, also John, also a gardener and plant collector, lived for a time at St Augustine's, occupied then by Lord Wotton, to whom he was loaned by the Cecil family. It was then (1619) that he sent his son to the King's School.

John the father subsequently joined the entourage of James I's favourite, the Duke of Buckingham, and went to Paris with Buckingham to attend the wedding by proxy of Charles I to Henrietta Maria. Besides plants, he collected curios, and one of these was the pair of boots of the court dwarf, Jeffrey Hudson, who caught the Queen's attention when he was served to her by the Duke of Buckingham inside a cold pie. Tradescant now left Canterbury and eventually settled in South Lambeth where he opened a museum of his curios, known as Tradescant's Ark. In 1630 he received his most important royal reward: appointment as Keeper of His Majesty's Gardens.

When he died in 1638 his son succeeded him as Charles I's gardener, and also took charge of his father's museum. And although between 1637 and 1654 he made three collecting expeditions to Virginia, it was to the care of the museum that he returned. Two years later he published its catalogue, dedicating this to the President and Fellows of the Royal College of Physicians. The current president of the college was the even-better-known King's School old boy, William Harvey, and it had been founded before the Reformation by Thomas Linacre (see page 9).

Tradescant died in 1662, leaving in his will his 'closet of rarities' to his wife for her lifetime then to the University of Oxford or Cambridge, but two years later his friend Elias Ashmole went to law, where the court accepted that a deed of gift from Tradescant to Ashmole was superior to the will. In 1677 Ashmole announced that he would give Tradescant's rarities to Oxford University, where these formed the basis of the Ashmolean Museum. The following April Mrs Tradescant was found drowned in her garden pond.

If Tradescant, naturalist and collector – and indeed Harvey before him – suggest that the King's School in these years was producing men at the forefront of a new scientific approach to learning, the impression is confirmed by two other scholars of the time: John Bargrave, nephew of Dean Isaac Bargrave, also a collector who formed a private museum which the cathedral now keeps (his more famous exploit is described in the next chapter); and John Spencer, who in his book, *De Legibus Hebraeorum Ritualibus et earum Rationibus* (1685), was the first to set Judaism in the historical context of other middle-eastern faiths. Two hundred years later it was described as 'still . . . by far the most important book on the religious antiquities of the Hebrews'. In short, Spencer invented the subject of Comparative Religion.

Ludd finally died, still headmaster, in mid-September, 1649, less than nine months after Charles I's execution. He, like Raven before him, was succeeded by his own lower master, Edward Browne (another King's Scholar). Almost at once Parliament ordered a survey of all lands and properties taken from the Deans and Chapters, which gives a detailed description of the headmaster's house. It stood in the Mint Yard adjoining the school and had a hall, parlour, kitchen, washhouse, and wood house, all presumably on the ground floor, and six chambers no doubt

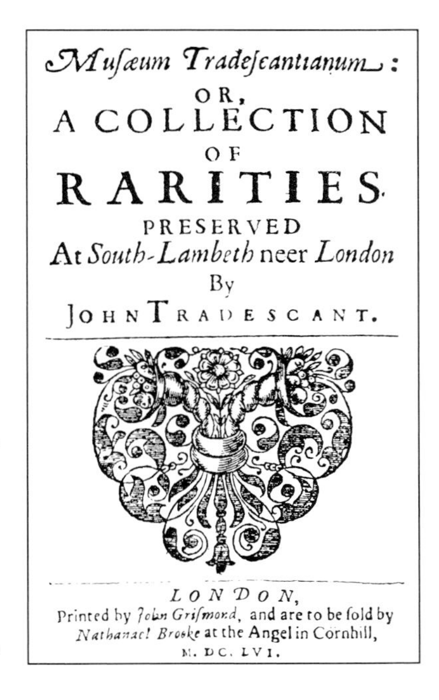
Musæum Tradescantianum:
OR,
A COLLECTION
OF
RARITIES
PRESERVED
At *South-Lambeth* neer *London*
By
JOHN TRADESCANT.

LONDON,
Printed by *John Grismond*, and are to be sold by *Nathanael Brooke* at the Angel in Cornhill,
M. DC. LVI.

The title page of the catalogue of Tradescant's Ark.

Sr: John Tradescant Junr:
in his Garden.

Mediterraneum

on the first floor; also an old kitchen. The lower master's house, again in the Mint Yard, had similar main rooms, but only five chambers and, it seems, no kitchen. While the headmaster had 'a little garden', the lower master had only 'a little garden spott'.

Though there is no surviving curriculum for the school in Ludd's or Browne's times, it was probably similar to that of Rotherham School as described in detail by its headmaster, Charles Hoole. This shows that by now Greek and Latin had established the total domination of British education which they retained for 200 years and partially retained for another hundred. True, the reading and writing of English was taught, but Hoole makes no reference to mathematics, modern languages, geography, or any history except Greek and Roman. Hebrew alone provided, for the sixth form, a little variety.

In Browne's time the school had no governing body, but, like a civil service with no government, it seems to have continued to function from force of habit. Browne was presumably acceptable to Cromwell's régime, though not a puritan sympathizer. Indeed, his wife, Barbara, was the daughter of a Kentish loyalist who had suffered much loss as a result of supporting the King, and when Browne died in 1658 she married that other well-known Royalist, William Somner. A Latin poem of Browne's survives which praises Somner. Clearly Browne moved in circles which were hostile to the government, but he, too, had connections with the city authorities which may have helped him to survive.

He was succeeded by a sterner puritan, Henry Montague. According to William Gostling, it was during Montague's time that the 'Dean's Great Hall' in the Green Court was 'demolished by the zealous Puritans for being profaned by the King's Scholars having acted plays there'. Certainly play-acting at the school, which had remained a tradition in the 1620s and 30s as the cathedral treasurer's grants show, was stopped by the puritans. And Hodgson's Hall, which now stands on the site, carries the date 1659 over its door. But the modern view is that the old hall merely collapsed of old age. If so, Gostling's suggestion is typical of the ways in which later historians blamed the puritans for damage they did not actually do.

Next year when the Restoration ended Montague's brief reign, he and his scholars were ejected one and all. By then the cathedral was, in Somner's words, 'more like a ruined monastery than a church'. It cost the Dean and Chapter £1000 to repair the organ which Sandys's troopers had wrecked, and Somner was given ten shillings for rescuing the font.

A generation after William Harvey three 17th century King's Scholars exemplify the rise of the modern Western outlook:

Top left: John Tradescant the Younger, gardener, plant-hunter, colonist and, with his father, founder of the first public museum in this country. (Oil by Emanuel de Critz.)

Top right: John Spencer, author of De Legibus Hebraeorum Ritualibus et earum Rationibus, *the founding work in the modern study of comparative religion. (Engraving from the* De Legibus, *1685.)*

Below: John Bargrave, traveller and as collector preceded only by the Tradescants. Matteo Bolognini's oil shows him in Sienna in 1647 with two young companions. Hand on heart is John Raymond, Bargrave's cousin and probably also a King's Scholar.

5

MR LOVEJOY AND THE RESTORATION

THE TOTAL EXPULSION OF THE SCHOOL'S SCHOLARS AT THE RESTORATION MAY NOT HAVE BEEN AS UNJUSTIFIED AS IT SOUNDS. ON MONTAGUE'S FINAL LIST, TWO OF THEM SIGNED only with their marks, for two their mothers signed, and for a fifth his mother made her mark. Justified or not, the school soon reassembled with an entirely new 50 scholars under a new headmaster, John Paris. But Paris's five years in office were in the nature of an interregnum, and it was only in 1665 that the next memorable headmaster arrived. He was the Revd George Lovejoy, who had been a chaplain in Charles I's army, then for 11 years headmaster of Islington School.

At the same time, on 13 April that year, the Dean and Chapter, as if determined to make a fresh start, issued 24 new Rules and Orders for the governing of 'the Freeschoole at Canterbury'. The 1665 rules give a vivid idea of the post-Restoration school, and of how it had changed in the century and a quarter since it was refounded.

In 1660 the Headmaster and the King's Scholars, deemed illegal interlopers, were expelled, with redundancy payments. The Lower Master had tactfully died but compensation was paid into his estate.

A remarkable number concern discipline – a comment no doubt on the previous five years. Boys were not to 'hurle, fling or sling stones', to bellow, hoot, or make 'any other unseemly noise', nor to indulge in 'overmuch noise and gabling' in schooltime, 'to swear, curse, bann, or use any lewd, or prophane language', to gamble or 'throw at Cocks', nor to play in any form in 'the Mint Yard, the Greencourt, the Church, Churchyard or Cloyster'. They were to be timed by the schoolmaster or usher when they went to the 'place of easement in the Forrains' to make sure they did not idle or loiter there. If scholars did break windows the cost of repair was to come from their 'wages'. If a commoner broke them and could not get a friend to pay for repairs he was to be expelled.

School hours were to be from 7 to 11 in the morning, and from 1 to 5 in the afternoon. When school ended both at 11 a. m. and 5 p. m. the boys were to be led by the master and usher to 'ye place called the Turnpike beside the prison door' and there 'go orderly and civilly away' hatless while in sight of the masters – 'unless in foul weather'. This Turnpike was not a road, but a spiked barrier at the entrance to the Mint Yard below the old North Hall (where the Dean and Chapter had a prison). In other words, the masters were to see the boys off the school premises but no further.

In school the masters were ordered to 'teach the boys no other but Classical Authors as Terence, Tully, Ovid, Virgil, Hor[ace], Homer, Isoc[rates] . . .' . Standards were notably lower than those required at the Reformation. Boys who had not learned to 'write or cipher' before coming to the school were told they must take lessons in these out of school hours.

The scholars were to provide themselves with purple gowns and with surplices; if they came to church not wearing these they were to be considered absent. Surplices were to be washed during the week so that they were clean for Sundays. For evening services on Sundays, holy days, and the eves of holy days, 'at the call of Bell Harry' (the bell which gives the cathedral's central tower its name) they were to assemble again at the Turnpike and be marched two by two to church, the monitors marching alongside like platoon sergeants.

In church they were not to allow any woman or other person to take their stalls, and during the sermon, to prevent themselves from 'gazing and slooping', they were to take written notes.

The new orders were signed by William Somner, who, after the Restoration, had become auditor to the Dean and Chapter. He may himself have drafted them (with help perhaps from his new wife, headmaster Browne's widow) and if so they represent another attempt to restore to his old school the standards it had had when he was there.

George Lovejoy came to Canterbury with recommendations from the headmasters of the Merchant Taylors' School and of St Paul's. Both said that he was a good teacher and, equally important, that he was religiously orthodox. 'Sincerely conformable to ye Church of England in doctrinals and rituals', John Goad of the Merchant Taylors' wrote. Lovejoy's enjoyment of his new job is demonstrated by a unique record of the school which he kept, conveniently called *Mr Lovejoy's Book of Speeches* – though he gave it a 42-word title in Latin. In it he recorded the performances of the boys on the school's four annual speech days. These marked

The Dark Entry and Bell Harry in winter.

Charles II's birthday and Restoration Day (29 May), the discovery of the Gunpowder Plot (5 November), the winter breaking-up of the school, and the approach of Lent (see *Plate 6*).

Most were in Latin and expressed appropriately loyal sentiments. But others were in English and were in the nature of what would be now called sketches, and some of these were less conformist, giving a boys' picture of the school to complement the picture given by the Dean and Chapter's 1665 'Rules and Orders'.

In winter, when the nominal purpose of the speeches was to ask for a short holiday *before* Christmas, they included many complaints about the schoolroom itself. A typical speaker says, 'I cannot tell the audience how much we suffer from the cold . . . . The ink freezes in one boy's inkhorn, the very brains freeze in the head of another. Our teeth chatter, we hit out at one another in an insane fashion. We are constrained to warm our frozen fingers with the breath of our mouths because *as you see there is here neither fire nor fireplace*. Some of us have such bad chilblains that we can neither run nor jump; besides, we do not dare to make a noise in school, lest the monitors should report us to the masters . . .'.

Reaching this icy cavern by seven on a winter morning was also a problem, and a boy might arrive like a 'human sponge, drenched with filthy water discharged from the upper windows of the houses, while . . . he was gazing upwards as though directing his course by the stars'. Or in the darkness he might run his head into some pillar or buttress, arrive with a black eye, and be punished by the master for fighting with street boys.

Corporal punishment was normal, and a master given the name of Yrkham (no doubt for his character) is said to be 'a shrewd Tanner of boys' fleshy parts'. A father, leaving a crying boy at school, is made to say, 'Peace, my good child. Thy mother will send thee a Crock of Butter and some Honey to sweeten thy lipps after Mr Yrkham has done with thee, And I will come every Saturday . . .'.

The same father tells the headmaster that he has modest academic ambitions for his son. 'I desire your destruction (*sic*) neither to make him a prating Brocter, nor vaunting Priest, nor lying Lawyer nor Physician Killman. Let him but read his accidunce, and be able to read a chapter to mee and my Dame by the fireside when we are both asleep, and it will be book learning enough.' But when he uses these arguments to haggle about the fees the master tells him to pay two pounds sterling a year 'or take away your son as you brought him hither'.

The boys considered their work load excessive. 'O ye . . . governors of this school', one speaker appeals, 'have pity on our minds exhausted by studies often prolonged into the long watches of the night, on our bodies racked with cold, on our clothes all frayed, patched, and torn, in fact quite worn out, through long exile from home.'

In another 'dialogue' eight students discuss their future careers. One wants to go into the Church.

'Faith!' another answers, 'I thought soe. For thou lookst as gravely as if thou stoodst for a lecture shortly, and wert for Thirty pounds a year once a week to preach the parish asleep. . . . Get but a competent impudence, a whining tone, an uncouth face, and a clubb fist to thump well, and a she zealott's call; and thy auditory shall be as much crouded as a montebank's stage. . . .'

Another wants to be a doctor.

PLATE 5

Left: Serenade in the Cloisters, one of the concerts in King's Week.

Below: The Norman arches under the Schoolroom, for centuries the mustering place of the King's Scholars.

PLATE 6

The Royal coat of arms in Lattergate garden was probably placed there to celebrate the Restoration of Charles II in 1660.

A King's Scholar made this drawing to illustrate an allegory acted in about 1680. His Hebrew runs the wrong way. It is preserved in Mr Lovejoy's Book of Speeches.

'O, you'll be a hipocriticall Physician, a learned tormentor, a lingering executioner to death that strives by art to make men long in dying.'

Another wants to go to the university and is warned not to do things during the long vacation that might make him blush 'for former exploits' when he returns.

More surprising than the boys' complaints and rebellious attitudes, which could be paralleled in most schools in most ages, is that the headmaster should so carefully have copied them down. His large folio volume of 'speeches' is preserved in the cathedral library.

The boys do not complain about the school's sanitary arrangements, as they probably might have done, but on the first recorded Speech Day (November 1655) the plague is once again said to be approaching Canterbury, causing the more timid parents to keep their boys at home. Soon afterwards the school had a case, and the auditor (William Somner) ordered him to be isolated in a tent on the 'Dungell', then waste land, later the Dane John. Here he was given straw for a bed, and wine, saffron, and ointment as medicines, while a maidservant brought him food. But after 12 days he died and was carried to his grave by the 'Searcher and Beadle'.

The performances of the week before Lent were different, taking the form of debates, sometimes conducted in extemporary verse, between scholars and commoners. At their conclusion two victors were chosen by popular vote. The victors had useful privileges: they had leave to study at home or to visit absent friends whenever they wished. By composing exercises in verse they could save special friends from being beaten in Lent. They could obtain for four friends who had done them special favours afternoon holidays on Mondays, Wednesdays, and Fridays. And by giving the headmaster copies of verses on every Tuesday and Thursday they could get a half holiday for the whole school.

On Charles II's birthday and Restoration Day, loyalty to the school and king were the predominant themes. Typically Ned, an old boy (though not, one would hope, a scholar) is made to tell his friend Knobs what he thinks of the occasion. 'O excellent, O how excellently have these pretty children told what my heart did burn to declare. That is what happiness we enjoyed under Charles the First, whom rebels by murder made glorious. And what grievances we groaned under in the absence of our sovereign (whom God be blessed we now enjoy) when he passed from that faithful oak to foreign nations. And, neighbour Knobs, neighbour Knobs, what grievances and woes did we then groan with under that heavy rump Parliament, what vengeance then did we suffer from Sequestration and slavery from those whom foolish volk call'd Liberty keepers, but I say, pardon the word, Liberty pounders.'

Knobs also complains of his sufferings during the Civil War and Commonwealth. 'I then lost all, nay more than all, my butter crock and all, not so much as a wooden spoon or shoe or stockin left for my poor wife. . . .' Ned continues in the same strain, ending 'thou knowest what Oakes blew Dick cut down and left not so much as a piece of timber to hang him and his fellow rebels'. Memories of Richard Culmer, alias Blue-skin Dick of Thanet, were much alive.

The boys also sometimes performed the works of professional dramatists, and Lovejoy's book lists the titles of a number of now-forgotten Restoration dramas. After this had been going on for some 17 years the Dean and Chapter seem to have noticed that such plays were not always edifying and ordered that 'No plais to be acted in the schoole unless first seene and allowed by the Deane or in his absence the Vice-Deane or in the absence of them both by the Senior Prebend present'.

This order taking censorship out of the headmaster's hands confirms what Lovejoy's book itself suggests, that he had become over-permissive. It was the tenth and final order in a list which suggests that he had been misbehaving in other ways. The first four limit the fees the boys should pay and conclude 'no other impositions whatsoever [may be charged] without the leave of the Dean and Chapter'. Number eight orders that no scholars be admitted without an examination by the master – an order presumably repeated only because it was not being observed. Number nine gives the Dean and Chapter rather than the headmaster the responsibility for promoting boys from the lower to the upper school. Lovejoy was now over 70 and when the Dean and Chapter suggested that he should leave he went quietly, to a parish on the Isle of Thanet – though perhaps unwillingly. When his rich wife died she left bequests to various charities but not to the King's School.

Early in his headmastership, Lovejoy had contributed £1 to a gallant and charitable project of John Bargrave, mentioned earlier for his museum of curios. Bargrave had been ejected from his Cambridge fellowship in 1643 and spent the next 17 years travelling in Europe before returning at the Restoration and becoming a Six Preacher of the cathedral then a canon (holding what had once been his uncle Dean Isaac's stall). He also became rector of Harbledown and of Pluckley, the parish which had caused Sir Edward Dering so much trouble. Bargrave's project was the rescue of the 300 British slaves, who, he estimated, were being held by Algerian pirates. Algerian pirates were the terrorists of the time. In 1621 the official purpose of the Mediterranean expedition which the elder John Tradescant had made was to fight them, though it was their 'apricocks' and gladioli rather than their bodies or slaves which he brought home. Bargrave does not seem to have taken the modern view that ransoming kidnap victims merely encourages the kidnappers – on the contrary, he and the Church raised the colossal sum of £10 000 for the purpose, to which the school contributed a total of £96 10*s* 3*d*.

'An Italian Slave, a Painter, drew me this rude piece' of Shaban Aga 'The King of Argeers', noted John Bargrave.

In his museum catalogue Bargrave describes how he 'bought [the prisoners] slave by slave from each particular Turkish patron, as one buyeth horses in Smithfield'. His principal dealings were with Shaban Aga, King of 'Argeers'. The king, sitting 'cross-legged on a Turkey carpet on a bench' was 'mostly very courteous' to Bargrave, sitting by him 'with my hat on, in my clerical habit', but at one stage 'we were both very hot and had like to have broken the peace, but at length reason prevailed'. Even when all the 162 ransomed slaves had been embarked on a British man-of-war, Bargrave reckoned that 'it was a thousand to one but that the peace between us had been broken, and I and my fellow commissioner, Dr Selleck, had bin made slaves'.

John Selleck, Archdeacon of Bath, had been unhelpful throughout. He had never been abroad before, Bargrave writes, could not 'speak a word of their language, and so understood not his danger until it was over'. The aftermath of Bargrave's heroic rescue demonstrates all too clearly the two men's danger. Though the British consul, Mr Browne, with whom Bargrave had stayed, 'had their *Lingua Franca* perfectly, . . . we were no sooner gone but they seized on all he had, shaved his head, and made him a slave, where he helped to draw timber and stones to a fortification, receiving so many blows a day with a bull's nerve, until he was beaten to death, and his body cast out upon a dunghill'.

When the Dean and Chapter replaced George Lovejoy, they confirmed in a letter to the archbishop that they had found the school 'sensibly declining by reason of the Head-master's age'. To succeed him they appointed Richard Johnson, who for three years had been lower master. They had had, they wrote, 'some years' tryall' of Johnson's 'skill and diligence'; they believed that the school had already improved and that 'In a short time it will recover its ancient reputation'.

Johnson had proved satisfactory for about five years, when the Dean and Chapter made three complaints within six months about him. They made the first in December 1688, the month after William of Orange had landed at Torbay and driven James II from the throne. Clergymen and schoolmasters were allowed till the following 1 August to take an oath of allegiance to the new King and those who refused became known as non-jurors. Johnson became a non-juror, and his refusal to swear, rather than his incompetence was probably why on 3 August 1699 the Dean and Chapter declared his position vacant.

Eighteen years later (1707) Johnson was appointed headmaster of the Free School at Nottingham. Again all went well at first but in 1718 the school governors tried to replace him, claiming that he was neglecting his duties and had become 'Delirious and Non Compos Mentis'. It was true that since coming to Nottingham Johnson had become involved in a violent controversy about a new edition of Horace by Richard Bentley, but he denied the charges, and had certainly been sensible enough to obtain from his employers a certificate of his competence to teach (saying that he needed it to apply for a new position). This he produced in court. When the Governing Body's counsel suggested to Johnson that 'much learning hath made thee mad', Johnson suggested to the court that at least the counsel 'would never be mad for the same cause'. His defence was good enough to persuade the City Corporation to pay him a pension for life provided he left. Three years later he was found drowned, but there is no reason to think that he committed suicide, or that he was madder than any other absent-minded academic.

The Dean and Chapter had now had to remove two headmasters in succession, and took trouble with their next selection, only appointing Thomas Atkins 'after some Tryall'. He was not yet in holy orders though he had taken them before his death 11 years later in 1700. By then he was still only 38 and his wife survived him by 55 years. Little else is known about Atkins. Though he was not apparently a distinguished headmaster, there was at one time a tablet in the Cathedral Cloisters which claimed that he 'left behind him a character hardly to be equalled'.

One hundred and sixty years had now passed since Henry VIII's refounding of the school, years during which religious controversy had caused two civil wars and several revolutions. As a semi-religious institution, the school could well have been regularly and seriously disrupted. The fact that it was not argues strongly that it was fulfilling a function for city and county which remained constant whatever religious or political party was in control. This in the end proved more important for its future than the temporary decline of its reputation under Lovejoy in his old age and under his successor.

6

THE EIGHTEENTH CENTURY

MATTHAEI RADERI
DE SOCIETATE IESV,
AD
M. VALERII
MARTIALIS EPI-
GRAMMATON
LIBROS OMNES,
PLENIS COMMENTARIIS,
NOVO STVDIO CONFECTIS, EX-
PLICATOS, EMENDATOS,
illustratos,
Rerúmque & verborum, lemmatum item, & communium locorum varijs & copiosis INDICIBVS *auctos,*
CVRÆ TERTIÆ,
Plurimis locis meliores.
David Jones
MOGVNTIÆ,
Sumptibus IOANNIS KINCKII, Bibliop. Colon.
Excudebat Hermannus Meresius.
Anno M. DC.XXVII.
Cum autoritate Superiorum, & privil. S. Cæs. Maiest.

Rader's edition of Martial's Epigrams *(Mainz, 1627) was among the books presented in 1702 by David Jones, whose signature appears in it, to the School library. A scholar has doodled on the unicorn.*

THE PATTERN FOR THE KING'S SCHOOL'S FORTUNES IN THE EIGHTEENTH CENTURY HAD BEEN SET BEFORE IT BEGAN. AS WITH OTHER COUNTRY GRAMMAR SCHOOLS, ITS REPUTATION and numbers improved when it had a good headmaster and declined when it had a bad one. Under the energetic Welshman, David Jones (1700–13), it prospered.

In 1702 Jones gave the school a large number of classical books, which still survive in its library. Previous histories of the school have argued that, with this gift, Jones founded the school library, but it is difficult to believe that for a century and a half the boys had had no access to books beyond their texts. Perhaps, like external users, they had access to the cathedral library – the fact that *Mr Lovejoy's Book of Speeches* ended there suggests this – or they may have had their own library to which Jones's gift was merely an important contribution.

Ten years later, probably with Jones's encouragement, the King's School Feast Society was founded. At first this was just an old boys' association. Members were to meet for an annual day of reunion which would include a sermon by an appropriate preacher, sometimes the headmaster. In 1718, however, the society took on another purpose: the raising of funds by a collection on each Feast Day for the support of exhibitions for King's Scholars at universities. For a century and a half the society carried out this useful function. How its Feast Days developed will be described presently.

Jones, however, like other headmasters of the period, had a problem. Besides being head of the school they usually held the livings of one or more parishes. Though these were mostly in Kent this nevertheless meant that on Sundays they would be away from Canterbury, conducting services in their parish churches. The parish which distracted Jones was Upper Hardres, five miles from Canterbury, and here he also went for some weeks at harvest time to collect his tithes. When the dean complained about Jones's long absences, Jones replied,

'Honoured Sir, – That I may not again give offence by being absent in Harvest, I am willing to resign my Mastership of the School; and accordingly I do hereby request, that you and the Reverend the Chapter will be pleased to accept of this my Resignation . . .'.

Two headmasters named Smith followed and the school's reputation declined. There was competition to succeed the second Smith, and the applications of three of the candidates note this decline. William Burroughs, lower master under the

Smiths, wrote that he had 'drudged full six years at the lower end' of the school. He was as a result 'the chief sufferer by, yet not chargeable with ye ruin of ye school, the declension of which had been owing in great measure to a slackness in point of discipline'.

Richard Bate, of Ashford Grammar School, in his application wrote that potential parents were hesitating to send their boys to Canterbury until they knew who was to be Smith's successor. If *he* was appointed this would not only reassure them because he 'had an interest with ye gentlemen of ye neighbourhood', but would have a more important advantage since 'he would remove good part of the Ashford school to Canterbury'. This was not an unknown thing to do at the time and could hardly have shocked the Dean and Chapter in the way Shirley shocked the Headmasters' Conference in 1935 (see page 91).

The third to offer himself was none other than the ex-headmaster, David Jones. To Archbishop Wake Jones wrote that in spite of what he had done for the school it was 'now sunk to so low a degree of Contempt and Disrepute, that some of those few Gentlemen's Sons, who are still in it, wou'd very likely have left it, if I had not prevented'. But Jones made a condition: that he should become a canon of the cathedral. He was clearly a man of insight, realising that a headmaster needed such a position to give him the power 'to do some service to the poor Schole of Canterbury'. More than 200 years were to pass before Shirley in 1935 was granted the same condition. In 1721 the Dean and Chapter rejected Jones as well as the other two applicants.

They chose instead the Revd John Le Hunt, an old Etonian who had graduated from King's College, Cambridge, then been headmaster of Brentford Grammar School. Under Le Hunt the school prospered again, to such an extent that in 1727 the Dean and Chapter were able to raise the entrance qualifications, ordering that candidates for scholarships must have spent a year at the school as commoners or must be over 13 years old. Numbers also increased and the school needed more accommodation for boarders. To provide this the Dean and Chapter in 1730 evicted one Mary Fuller from her house in the Mint Yard and surrendered a room above where the auditor had been living.

Le Hunt had held office for three years when an incident occurred which suggests that, successful headmaster though he may have been, he was a man of short temper, touchy about his reputation. To the vice-dean and prebendaries he complained on 20 March 1726 that in the Green Court James Turner, one of the cathedral's two vesturers, 'had uttered reproachful and opprobrious language' against him 'in the presence of several of his Scholars'.

Turner defended himself in a remonstrance which gives a circumstantial account of the incident. '. . . after evening prayers I was walking in the Green Court; the said Mr Le Hunt's Boarders, whether with a design to mobb me or no I leave to yor judgements, but insult me they did after this manner. "Here comes the Pedlar, Who wants any Pictures?" which was immediately answered among themselves, "Who has any to sell?" And that was again readily answered "Domine Turner Dom Turner" . . . . This continued for about an hour or more without ever a word from me as yet being surprised at their rude behavior. By and by Mr Ladd the Gardener came into the Green Court and I beckoned and desired to speak with him. . . . Mr Ladd stood amazed as well as myself, and said these Boys are certainly encouraged and put upon this malicious spight and outrage. At last I bespoke to Powel by name saying, You Rascal, does your Master allow you to treat me thus? which was the substance of all I said. . . .'

Le Hunt had next appeared from the Dark Entry, and some of the boys, Turner continues, had 'run to him and whispered, and by what followed it must be their telling him I called him Rascal, for I was no sooner got home than he was after me with his Attendants swollen with anger and rage, loading me with reproaches and threatenings as the vilest fellow upon earth, so that the neighbourhood rang out. Mr De Goss came by at the same time . . . I understand that he has taken so much notice of it as to wonder at seeing a clergyman in such a fury for nothing . . .'.

Turner admitted that he had made money by printing and selling heraldic engravings and 'also the works of the famous Andrea Palladio's Architecture'. His story seems credible, but the court found that it compounded his offence, since it contained 'many opprobrious reflections upon Mr Le Hunt with insinuations of his being unjust, avaricious and proud'. They ordered Turner to ask Le Hunt's pardon, either in writing or in public. Perhaps they knew more of Turner's character than the records spell out. He had, it seems, been taking a seat in the cathedral which implied that he was of equal standing with the school's two masters. He was ordered no longer to do this but 'to content himself with such a seat or place in our Quire as befits a Vesturer of this Church'.

Le Hunt also held a country living: the parish of Brookland on Romney Marsh. As with Jones, it was probably this which led to the end of his headmastership, though more dramatically. Riding, most likely to take a Sunday service there, he fell from his horse and was killed.

His successor, John Frances, had been a scholar under David Jones, indeed when Jones retired to Upper Hardres he had asked to have Frances as his curate because he didn't want to have to preach twice a day on Sundays. Frances had been another rejected applicant for the job of headmaster when Le Hunt was chosen, but he had subsequently become lower master. Now in 1731 he was appointed head. Besides being a Greek and Latin scholar, Frances had 'some knowledge of Oriental languages, at least of Hebrew'. Perhaps he and George Sale, a commoner of David Jones's time, who later made the first (and still best) translation of the Koran into English, had learnt together.

It was 50 years since the Dean and Chapter, towards the end of Lovejoy's time, had last issued orders and regulations for the school, and three days after appointing Frances they issued new ones. These were not comprehensive, but designed to correct specific abuses. They chiefly concerned the behaviour of the masters who were ordered not to appoint assistants without the dean and chapter's agreement, not to grant Playdays without the Dean, Vice-dean or senior prebendary's agreement, and not to demand a gratuity of more than 5 shillings from the boys at the end of terms. They were also to fill vacant scholarships strictly in order. It sounds as if parents with influence had been arranging for their sons to jump the queue.

When Frances died, after only three years in office, the Revd James Evans, his lower master, included in his epitaph a description of his character which translates 'He was a strong man among weak, tenaciously holding to what he believed right'. Soon afterwards the Revd John Lynch who had been Frances's schoolfellow and who had become dean the same year, had this sentence chiselled out. The dean had asked Frances for his 'vote', and Frances had refused it. Who or what the dean wanted him to vote for is not known – it could have been for some parliamentary candidate the dean favoured.

The same lower master, Evans, is mentioned in one of three surviving letters which eleven-year-old Edward Martin sent his mother (Honoured Madam) during headmaster Frances's time. His younger brother, Martin writes, 'is so very idle that Mr evens doth not no what to do with him'. The Martins – great-grandsons of General Fairfax – came from Loose near Maidstone and must have been commoners because they are not listed as scholars. Edward's letters consist mainly of what were probably more than merely formal inquiries and reports about his own and his family's health. 'I am a great deell better than I was when papa was heare,' he writes, 'and I hope you are all well. I drink milk every night and morning.' And 'I should [be] glad if you would [send] me and my brother a white wascoat.' As a Postscript he asks for 10 shillings a quarter for 'daunsing'.

Honred madam 1733

I am a great deell better than
I was when papa was heare,
and I hope you are all well,
I drink milk every night
and morning, and I hope papa
got home well, monday was the
first day of my going to skole,
my brothe is so very idle that
mr evens doth not no what to do with hem,
I am your dutifue son
Edward Martin

Edward Martin died in early manhood. His brother Denny, perhaps the idler of this letter, inherited Leeds Castle.

John Lynch was a commoner at the School in the early 1700s. He married one of Archbishop Wake's daughters in 1728 and was appointed Dean of Canterbury in 1734.

Frances was succeeded by the Revd Richard Monins, certainly of the same Kentish family as the treasurer, Capt Thomas Monins, who had supported the school during the Civil War. Monins must have known Frances as a boy, since he had been elected a King's Scholar only a year later. He had been headmaster for seven years when, on Guy Fawkes Day, 1743, a curious event occurred. That night the school performed Addison's play, 'Cato', not in the schoolhouse, where they used to perform plays in Lovejoy's time, but in the city's playhouse. The dean and prebendaries attended, and during the performance were so threatened by the city mob that troops had to be called to protect them. The Treasurer's book reports the incident: 'Given to the soldiers who guarded the Playhouse Novr 5, to keep off the mob from rushing on the Dean and Prebends, whilst the King's Scholars were acting before them the Tragedy of Cato'.

Perhaps the mob was merely overexcited on this day of celebration. Or it may have disliked Dean Lynch. A contemporary pamphlet by 'A Yeoman of Kent' suggests reasons why it might have been done. The dean's constant companions, the yeoman claims, were 'the Singing Men of his Cathedral', whom he allowed 'to govern his Family, and insult his Servants' though they bore 'the most infamous characters'. Furthermore, 'the tragical Storys of Mr Roberts, and of Ladd the Chorister, and their *Suspicious Deaths*' were well known. 'The indecent Kindness of Mr D__n for the one and his inhuman treatment of the other is beyond Example. . . . The Person of Ladd was his wanton Delight in all Companys'; and Mr Roberts he had starved in a garret 'confined upon the Pretence of Idiocy, to merit a Legacy from the rich old Mrs Pytie'.

Two letters from early in Monins' time suggest even more vividly than young Edward Martin's, the health hazards of eighteenth-century boarding schools. Both are addressed to a parent, Richard Tylden, and are about the illness of his son, fifteen-year-old Richard Osborne Tylden. One is from headmaster Monins himself, the other from Dr Christopher Packe, the doctor Monins called when the boy's illness seemed too serious to be treated by an apothecary. Though both gentlemen are concerned about the boy, both seem more concerned to quarrel about their respective apothecaries. Monins complains that Dr Packe has dismissed his own, Mr Chandler, and appointed another, Mr Hayward. Dr Packe suggests that Tylden 'will be inclin'd to think it is of much more consequence to have the apothecary agreeable to the Physician than to ye School master'. He has, he writes, 'so much reason to complain of the arbitrary and injurious providings at that school . . . it is no wonder if I should be averse to the new masters young apothecary'. Packe suspected smallpox and ordered a vomit, which Monins admitted 'worked with Him pretty well', and the boy was apparently recovering. The Packes were Canterbury doctors for several generations. Though Christopher Packe in his remedies was a doctor of his time, he seems to have had a more modern approach than some of his contemporaries, adding as a postscript to his letter that he would have said something more positive about the boy's fever 'but whether by design (which I am most inclined to think) or by supine negligence . . . the night water was thrown away, and no account of it given'.

By 1745 Monins' own health had deteriorated and he took leave of absence, then resigned. He seems to have been a satisfactory headmaster. The same cannot be said of the Revd Robert Talbot, his successor. Talbot was over 50 at this date so it seems possible that his appointment was an example of Canterbury nepotism. He was Dean Lynch's brother-in-law, having married the dean's sister Anne some 19 years earlier. During his three years of office the reputation of the school declined to one of its lowest points. By 1749 not only had its numbers fallen from 90 to 58, but only 18 boys were in the top half of the school. Talbot had not allowed this to happen by accident. He argued that if there were more in his own class he would have to employ an assistant, and paying an assistant would reduce his salary to less than that of the lower master.

More seriously, he was considered, even in those rough times, to be unacceptably brutal. In November the same year a parent, Samuel Shepherd, complained that his son Julius had been subjected to 'dangerous and forbidden correction given him by Mr Talbot, Chief master of the King's School, namely, by kicking him on ye belly at one time, and beating him at another with an hazel stick till he broke it on him'.

Others besides Shepherd disliked Talbot. One of the prebendaries, Dr Downe, had had a violent quarrel with him which resulted in such a 'great spite' against him that he is said to have encouraged the sending of a particularly 'daring refractory clever boy' to the school 'who would be sure to torment' Talbot. The boy was Edward Thurlow, later Lord Chancellor. According to Sir Egerton Brydges, a subsequent King's Scholar with whom this story originates, Thurlow co-operated with the doctor's plan, 'leading a life of torment to his master, Talbot, by his tricks and drolleries'. On the other hand, the Revd J. S. Sidebotham, in his 1865 account of the school, claims that in later life Thurlow 'always spoke kindly of Mr Talbot'. Indeed Thurlow later became briefly related by marriage to Talbot. In 1760 he seduced and, according to his latest biographer, probably married Kitty Lynch. Kitty was Dean Lynch's youngest daughter, and thus was Talbot's wife's niece.

Whatever part Dean Lynch may have played in the appointment of his brother-in-law, by the end of 1749 he must have seen that this had been a mistake. He now sent Talbot a list of questions about his teaching and punishing practices. In reply to the question, 'What books are read in the School?', Talbot detailed the authors which the 'Little Classes', 'Next Class', 'Third Class', 'Fourth Class' and 'Head Form' read, and the exercises they did. Greek began in the 'Next Class'. One of the exercises in the Fourth Class was translating Horace's odes into English verse. About punishments Talbot seems to have been in some confusion. He admitted to 'A Rod' and 'a slap of the face, confinement, and proper punishment as deserved', but the phrases 'sometimes a box o' th' ear' and 'except once a boy was struck with a stick that he was doing mischief with' were struck out. When Talbot appealed to the Archbishop, Dr Herring decided that the complaints of the Dean and Chapter were justified.

Edward Thurlow, Lord Chancellor under North and Pitt, and the only man for whom Dr Johnson polished his conversation beforehand. (Engraving after T. Phillips, 1800.)

Soon afterwards (22 February 1750) the vice-dean and treasurer were sent to inspect the school. They found the 'undermaster' and the 'Assistant to the Upper Master' (in spite of his protests, Talbot had appointed one) 'attending upon their duties', but Talbot himself was missing, as he had been, they were told, for some time. He had returned a week late for the start of term and left again after 15

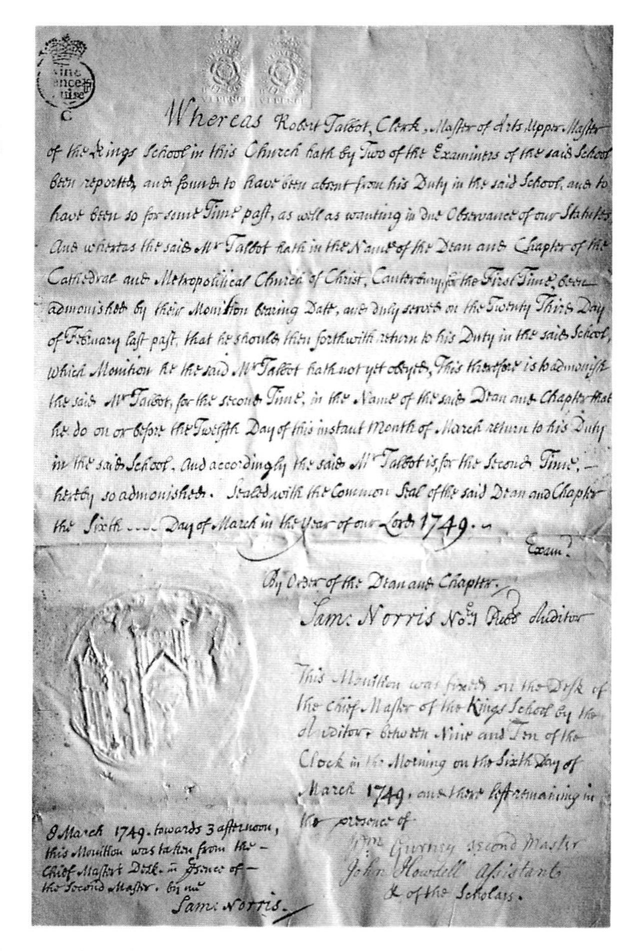

Whereas Robert Talbot, Clerk, Master of Arts Upper Master of the Kings School in this Church hath by Two of the Examiners of the said School been reported, and found to have been absent from his Duty in the said School, and to have been so for some Time past, as well as wanting in due Observance of our Statutes, And whereas the said Mr Talbot hath in the Name of the Dean and Chapter of the Cathedral and Metropolitical Church of Christ, Canterbury, for the First Time, been admonished by their Monition bearing Date, and duly served on the Twenty Third Day of February last past, that he should then forthwith return to his Duty in the said School, which Monition he the said Mr Talbot hath not yet obeyed, This therefore is to admonish the said Mr Talbot, for the second Time, in the Name of the said Dean and Chapter that he do on or before the Twelfth Day of this instant Month of March return to his Duty in the said School. And accordingly the said Mr Talbot is, for the Second Time, hereby so admonished. Sealed with the Common Seal of the said Dean and Chapter the Sixth .... Day of March in the Year of our Lord 1749.

Exam[illegible]

By Order of the Dean and Chapter.
Sam: Norris No[illegible] Pub[illegible] Auditor

This Monition was fixed on the Desk of the Chief Master of the Kings School by the Auditor between Nine and Ten of the Clock in the Morning on the Sixth Day of March 1749, and there left remaining in the presence of
Wm Gurney Second Master
John Howdell Assistant
& of the Scholars.

8 March 1749. towards 3 afternoon, this Monition was taken from the Chief Master's Desk in presence of the Second Master, by me
Sam: Norris.

Robert Talbot was warned three times about neglecting his duties as 'Upper Master of the King's School'. This, the second monition, was 'fixed to his desk between Nine and Ten of the Clock in the Morning of the Sixth Day of March 1749'.

days. The auditor was therefore ordered to fix a 'Monition' to Talbot's desk. If, after this had been three times repeated, Talbot still ignored it, his position would be declared vacant. Talbot perhaps complied, but on 2 May that year he resigned.

Dean Lynch made a better choice when he replaced his brother-in-law with Dr Osmund Beauvoir. Beauvoir's family had probably come from France in Henry II's reign, though his particular branch had later settled in Guernsey. The name was occasionally written Beaver, and probably pronounced that way. He was a close friend of Hasted, the historian of Kent, and Hasted is fulsome in Beauvoir's praise, describing him as 'a gentleman, whose merit no expressions of mine can either flatter, or transmit to posterity . . .'. He brought the school, Hasted says, to 'the highest degree of estimation'. Not surprisingly, Hasted sent his son there. Sir Egerton Brydges (quoted above about Thurlow), who was one of Beauvoir's pupils, writes in his autobiography that Beauvoir was 'one of the most correct classical scholars of his day . . . a man of real genius . . . to whom the present writer owes all that he knows of the learned languages'. Brydges adds that 'Two versifications from Isaiah and Jeremiah, which I wrote for school-tasks at Christmas 1777, my age fifteen, and which gained great applause, fixed my ambition to write verse for life'.

Though Brydges published novels as well as verse, he was, in the sober words of the *Dictionary of National Biography*, 'unhappily led to mistake his delight in reading great works of literature for an evidence of his capacity to produce similar works himself'. He also spent much time trying, but failing, to prove that his elder brother was the rightful Lord Chandos. On the other hand, his editing and publishing of rare works at Lee Priory Press 'rendered a service to the students of old English Literature', particularly of Elizabethan times.

Another would-be poet from Beauvoir's time was George-Monck Berkeley, son of a canon of the cathedral, grandson of the philosopher, Bishop Berkeley. When George-Monck died young in 1793, his mother, Elizabeth Berkeley, published 200 of his not very distinguished poems, appended to a 630-page introduction by herself. She was a flamboyant lady, the subject of many Precincts stories, and features in several of those told by that excellent gossip of the next generation, George Gilbert. 'She was a vain conceited woman', Gilbert writes, 'and plain, and high shouldered. One day speaking of her dear self she said she was so handsome in her youth that she was quite annoyed by the importunities of her numerous suitors. So she took the door-key of her father's house and put it into her small mouth to stretch it and render herself plain. "And you did it *effectively*" observed Muff Bridges.'

Brydges considered her 'the most garrulous, vain, presumptuous, and ill-tempered woman'. When she was angry she 'would sit for hours relating a set of scandalous stories, all falsehoods her own fertile inventions from beginning to end'. And John Tucker, son of the lower master, reported in a letter to a Cambridge scholar that 'Mrs Berkeley and Mrs Preb. Benson have made a public exhibition in the Oaks lately; and I believe it was expected they would have gone to pulling of caps'.

Poor Mrs Berkeley had been unlucky with her children. Her younger boy, George Robert, had died at the school, aged 8 years and 4 months, of a putrid fever. She includes with her elder son's poems a verse epitaph for George Robert, written by a schoolfellow, together with footnotes of at least twice its length in praise of her saintly little boy. Senior scholars, Mrs Berkeley writes, were in the habit of cheating the local orange-selling woman by taking more than they paid for, but the trick required the help of a smaller boy, and one Samuel Sawbridge had refused to co-operate. When she asked her son if he 'should have been as honest as his dear friend Samuel?' he replied ' "God knows, my dear Mamma, if I had been tempted, what I *might* have done: THANK GOD, THANK GOD, they did not *ask* me." And he shuddered as he emphatically uttered the reply.'

To return to the worthy Dr Beauvoir, he is described by Cole in his *Athenae Cantabrigienses* as 'a cheerful companion [who] sang a good song and understood music well'. But he was not universally liked, as the diary of the Revd Joseph Price shows. Price was a country parson who held four livings in Kent, the first two overlapping, and eventually leased a house in the Mint Yard. He was neither well known to his contemporaries nor rich (he would list the financial advantages and disadvantages of girls he was considering marrying) and today he would be forgotten but for his diary which he kept, using the same shorthand Pepys used. Soon after three volumes of this had been found (1949) and transcribed (1953),

F. J. Shirley, then the school's headmaster, wrote that Price's diaries were 'In places . . . as interesting as Parson Woodforde's remarks; here and there . . . more eyebrow-raising than Samuel Pepys' observations'.

Price's gossip goes back to the start of Beauvoir's time, when the Revd William Gurney was lower master and provided accommodation for a few boarders. Gurney, Price writes, 'never had any hashes nor minces at his table, nor meat pies I think. The boys say they have the bones after the maids have picked them.'

This mild accusation of meanness is nothing compared to the comments he makes or quotes about Beauvoir. The headmaster, he claims, was 'brought up by Mrs Lynch' the dean's wife – and there were 'some disagreeable reports about the late *Dean's affection* for Beauvoir' – Dean Lynch once more. At Cambridge he had 'kept high and great company,' and 'lived as fellow in great pomp'. 'Don't like Beauvoir's pomp', Price writes, 'and being the Schoolmaster in company', while Price's neighbour calls Beauvoir 'an impudent, shewy, pushing, boshy, florid man', who would serve ostentatiously expensive dinner parties. 'Gave a most grand entertainment last Christmas to Dr Tatton and his lady. Green peas one dish. Had been preserved in salt till that time.'

Manby Tylden had boarded with John Tucker, the Lower Master, who died in 1776. Another master was nominally put in charge of the boys but Jane Tucker, the widow, obviously still ran things and presented this 1778 bill.

Beauvoir could probably afford such extravagances. He held three Kent livings: Littlebourne, Milton next Sittingbourne, and Iwade. He was a Six Preacher at the cathedral, and his first wife, Anne Boys, brought him £3000. Nevertheless, when she died he was keen, according to Price, 'to get Miss Knatchbull or to marry well somewhere'. But Price's attitude is ambivalent. While he observes that 'Beauvoir st.tches Mrs Hasted,' among his own social ambitions he includes, 'To be intimate with Beauvoir'. And the Precincts gossip which he reports is more than balanced by the evidence of Hasted and others that Beauvoir was the school's most successful headmaster of the eighteenth century.

He was in his sixties when he retired in 1782. A few days later he was created a Doctor of Divinity, and in October the same year he celebrated his retirement by marrying his second wife, Mary Sharpe.

An interesting school bill survives from Beauvoir's time (1778), paid for Manby Tylden, son of Dr Packe's patient Richard. The total for two quarters is substantial (£24 5*s* 4*d*) at a time when the headmaster's official salary was still only £20 a year. 'Board' is the largest item (£9), and after that various amounts for clothing, tailoring, and shoes which total £5 18*s* 9*d*. The bookseller gets £2 10*s* 6*d*, the writing master £1 3*s* 4*d*, the dancing master £1 9*s*, the barber 9*s* 3*d*, and the school sweep 3*s* 6*d*. The teaching fee is a modest £1 1*s* 7*d*, but there is a 'breaking up' fee of 10*s* 6*d*, which presumably went to head or lower master. Manby was a commoner so there is no scholarship deduction, though the form has space for one.

By the time Richard Tylden the elder was paying this bill, Manby's brother, Richard, was at Jesus College, Cambridge. He must have been a popular boy, because several school friends, including James Six and John Tucker (the future headmaster) sent him quite frequent letters there, with news of Canterbury. They give a vivid idea of what school life seemed like to boys of the time. Six's and Tucker's also make an interesting contrast.

Six's are full of envy for Tylden, now at the university. 'Indeed Dick', he writes, 'you wrong me when you suppose I can live happily at school without you! You envy me, you say: believe me, I have more cause to envy you since the novelty of your situation, the happiness of it . . . and the numerous acquaintances as well old as new which you will meet with at Cambridge, will abundantly compensate you for the loss [or] absence of one . . . .' What is more, Six tells Tylden, 'I HAVE GOT A GREEK SPEECH . . . . Mr Beauvoir (God bless him) – for I won't use bad names – on Monday morning presented me with one prose . . . . None of the others have as yet been given out so that I can give you no other information tho' I believe you have now enough to surprise you for a fortnight . . .'.

Osmund Beauvoir addresses a respectful young man in the Mint Yard. (Detail from a Francis Grose watercolour of 1767.)

Tylden must have answered with only modest enthusiasm about Cambridge, but Six persists. 'I cannot . . . forget the pleasing thought of having no stupid Greek epigrams to translate, no fifty line Virgil lesson to make nonsense of . . . .' Just the same he seems to have been an earnest boy, and asks Tylden to send him from Cambridge any 'studies of Logic and Algebra . . . which would instruct without puzzling'. 'We are all in high spirits,' he adds, 'on account of the approaching Holidays.'

By the time Six writes again (24 January 1774) he and his father have successfully visited Tylden at Cambridge. Back at school, however, he is 'in the same situation as before, employ'd in the same studies, bound by the same rules; nor do I seem to myself of greater importance except sometimes when the discourse is concerning the university, then I must say I am listen'd to with something more than ordinary attention'.

Six continues to ask anxiously for academic advice. He wants to know if there is an English translation of 'the funeral orations', and 'whose Algebra is used at Trinity'. When summer comes he pleads guilty to idleness, but 'must observe that in this delightful season a person must be deaf, blind, and indeed quite insensible not to be call'd forth by the loveliness of the season and the beauty of the flow'ry landscape.' But in July he reports that 'Tough Euclid I must obey out of fear, and venerable Homer out of love, and as for that intricate yet somewhat entertaining fellow Algebra, both love and fear enforce his orders'. And by October he is even mastering tough Euclid. 'I have done 24 Propositions,' he tells Tylden, '. . . The thirteenth which puzzled me a little I found prov'd in different manner by Barrow.' A drawing and the proof follow.

Untypically, on 19 August he has sent Tylden some gossip: their fellow student LeGeyt and a young lady 'went from Dover to Fernes and were married there. His father as soon as he suspected it took chaise for Dover and met them just as they came on shore after the expedition. Affairs were then settled in an amicable manner and the bridegroom is supposed to be with his spouse at her mother's in the Friars'.

Tucker's letters are nothing except gossip. 'Miss Beauvoir is absent', he writes, 'the Airsons set off for Ramsgate tomorrow; the Frends are soon going to Mr Tizard's, I cannot recollect the name of his habitation. Kitty has had an offer of Jack Curling's hand but she is rather above a farmer. . . . Cyprian Bunce lays close siege to her, and there is little room to doubt but she has already struck to him. I supp'd at Frend's last night. . . . Bunce could not resist the temptation of sitting next her [Kitty]. Miss Frend (contrary to the etiquette of the teatable) made tea. . . . Do you know Mrs Hopton, formerly Secker? Well, for fear you should not I'll tell you she is an old niggardly, stingy B__ch, she lives in Dr Sutton's house. The Dr. was down some time ago, and at his departure Mrs H[opton] sent him a bill of little articles among which was one for Emptying the bogs, 17 Shil. The Dr. had spirit enough to tell [her] they that fill'd it might empty it. . . .'

His next letter returns to the subject of Kitty, whom Tylden as well as Bunce seems to fancy. 'Oh Dick, what in love again? or are you jealous? so much in love that you want a recipe from such a novice as myself. I hope you'll have laid aside your ferocity before I return. The pistols are ready etc. I desire one favour which is I may have the honour of being your second, for of all the fools I ever saw I think Bunce the greatest.' By June 1777, however, Bunce has been successful for there is a Mrs Bunce, presumably Kitty. Tucker tells Tylden that 'she looks extremely well and very *matron-like* (much more so than I expected)'. Meanwhile, the unfortunate Miss Beauvoir 'hangs in hand yet, nor do I see any chance of her going off, without you will take compassion on her deserted beauty'.

Beauvoir did one service to the school for which anyone writing its history must be grateful; he began a school register, entering in it all those present when he arrived and all subsequent entrants. A comparison between its first 32 years when Beauvoir was headmaster and a similar period beginning about 80 years later (1833) tells us much about the way the service the school provided for Canterbury, Kent and the rest of the country changed over these years – the years of the Industrial Revolution.

During Beauvoir's period there are 633 entries (not counting re-admissions). For 584 of these the boy's place of birth is given and well over a third (about 210) were born in Canterbury. About another 260 were born in Kent, the largest group in Dover (25). A mere 34 were born in London, 59 in other parts of Britain outside Kent and 12 overseas. Put another way, only a little over a sixth of the boys had been born outside Kent.

During the later 32-year period there are almost exactly as many entries (645) but only half as many boys were born in Canterbury (about 110). Over twice as many had been born in what would now be called London (78), over twice as many in other parts of England outside Kent (150), and, most dramatic increase, five times as many overseas (59), mainly, but not exclusively, in parts of the world coloured red on the map. Now those locally born were only just over half the total. By 1865 it seems clear that the King's School was at least half-way from being a local grammar school to becoming a national 'public school'.

In Beauvoir's years information is given about the future lives of about 280 boys. Seventy-four went to Oxford or Cambridge. Perhaps others went there, among those about whom no information is given, but this probably represents the majority, because the headmaster would have been keen to record such successes. And only a proportion of those who went to Oxford or Cambridge would have taken holy orders. There seems, therefore, no justification for the suggestion that *most* boys of the school went into the Church. Of the 280, 25 became lawyers, 23 surgeons, 11 went into the army, 10 went into the navy or became farmers. In addition 13 became apothecaries and about another 30 became cabinet makers, upholsterers, butchers, bakers, grocers, etc., including one 'meal-man'.

These descriptions make another comparison possible: between boys with

In the 17th and 18th century King's School boys were allowed to play in the Cathedral Cloisters and many carved their names on the stone benches there. Charles Abbott, the future Lord Chief Justice, was one of them.

Charles Abbott, later Lord Tenterden, was made Lord Chief Justice of the King's Bench in 1818. (Engraving after J. W. Wright.)

clearly middle-class futures, including university entrants (154), and those with lower middle-class futures (43). The figures do not add up to 280 because occupations like merchant and brewer are ambiguous. The conclusion must be that at this time the school primarily served its locality, rather than a particular class. Again and again among its boys occur the names of prosperous Kentish families, who owned land in the county for many generations. At the school they mixed with the sons of Canterbury cobblers, weavers, bakers, and suchlike tradesmen of the city.

For some 250 boys their father's occupation is given and a high proportion (90) were clearly lower middle class. The implication might seem to be that many of the families who patronized the school would today be described as upwardly mobile. Certainly Charles Abbott, the best known of Beauvoir's pupils, was the second son of a wig-maker and hairdresser. John, the father, traded from a house just outside the western entrance to the cathedral, and had many of the cathedral's establishment as his customers; his son, Charles, was 'a grubby little boy who ran after his father, carrying for him a pewter basin, a case of razors, and a hair-powder bag'. But young Charles befriended the illegitimate son of another old King's Scholar, Lord Thurlow, who probably played a part in getting him a place at the school. Here 'his proficiency in Latin Verse was remarkable', and he became captain of the school. Meanwhile, his father had tried to get him accepted as a cathedral chorister, but fortunately the boy's voice was breaking and he was rejected. When he finished school his father wanted him to become an apprentice wig-maker and hairdresser. 'The indentures were actually signed, sealed and delivered' before the school made money available for him to go to Oxford. He subsequently climbed to the top of the legal profession, becoming Lord Chief Justice, and in 1827 Baron Tenterden.

But although Abbott was not unusual in having a lower middle-class father, he *was* a comparatively rare example of a tradesman's son rising into the professions. Of those 90 tradesmen's sons, only 11 others either did so or went to a university.

During the later 32 years (1833–65) about the same number of boys went to Oxford or Cambridge (63) and four went to London University – though it must be admitted that no fewer than 129 were *sons* of clerics. Among other boys from middle-class backgrounds, 90 were sons of army officers (a remarkable increase, no doubt caused by the opening of the barracks at Canterbury in 1794), 62 were sons of surgeons or physicians, 54 of farmers, 47 of lawyers, 16 of teachers, 12 of naval officers, 7 of bankers, 5 of architects, and 63 of fathers who merely called themselves gentlemen – a total, with the clerics, of 475.

There were again a number of fathers whose class is doubtful, but if these are set aside, about 70 boys remain whose fathers were definitely lower middle class. To some extent the King's School remained a provincial grammar school, catering for the sons of the tradesmen of Canterbury and Kent. On the other hand, it was now being overwhelmingly patronized by upper middle-class parents. In this sense, too, it was well on the way to becoming a national 'public school'.

PLATE 7

Above: The Memorial Court, Norman Staircase and Undercroft and over it the 1855 Schoolroom, Norman enough to have deceived several writers on architecture.

Left: The King's School drawn in 1777 by Francis Grose from his friend 'Mr Gosling's chamber window'. Minor Canon Gostling, an old King's Scholar, lived in the Northeast corner of the Mint Yard.

PLATE 8 Walking on the Green Court under 'the noblest tower in Christendom' after Sunday morning service.

7

DECLINE AND REVIVAL – NAYLOR TO WALLACE

JOHN TUCKER, WRITER OF THE GOSSIPY LETTERS QUOTED IN THE LAST CHAPTER, SUBSEQUENTLY LOWER MASTER, SUCCEEDED BEAUVOIR AS HEADMASTER IN 1782, BUT FOR ONLY THREE years. In 1785 he was followed by Christopher Naylor, who held office for 30 years. From Naylor's time we have memoirs of old King's Scholars to amplify the picture which boys' letters give of life at the school, in particular those of George Gilbert.

Gilbert, who often returned to Canterbury during his 30 years as second master of Grantham Grammar School, tells two tales which were current at the King's School when he first arrived there in 1808. One day a scholar, walking into Bell Harry tower and seeing a rope dangling from an aperture high above his head, gave it a tug. He did not realize that there was a deaf workman up there, to whom a tug on the rope was an order to wind in his winch. The rope began to rise and the boy hung on, thinking 'it was fun and that he would only draw him up a few yards and let him down. However, he soon found he was being gradually drawn up, and so held as tightly as he could. When the deaf man at length saw him, instead of landing him, he immediately in fear for the boy began to wind the rope back and to let him down. This rendered the danger double. He came, however, down without a fall. I have in vain tried', Gilbert adds, 'to discover the boy's name.'

On another occasion a scholar got locked into the cathedral one evening and settled down to sleep under the steps leading to the organ. 'About 9 o'clock however, Dr Buckworth . . . entered the Church . . . with his lantern and proceeded to the Library. The light as he passed cast its ray down the passage . . . the boy saw the glimmer, was affrighted and screamed out. The Doctor was surprized but advanced to discover whence the screams could proceed, found the alarmed boy, took him to his House, gave him refreshment, afterwards noticed and patronized him thro' life.' The freedom of the boys to wander in the cathedral is remarkable – though confirmed by cloister graffiti.

The school's official curriculum, according to Gilbert, still excluded all subjects except the classics. 'In my School days,' he writes, 'we could learn French privately as several did, and a master to teach writing and arithmetic attended for an hour

The arms of Australia and of The King's School, Parramatta, appear with those of the mother School on Lardergate in commemoration of Australian help with its rebuilding and extension in 1951.

daily. Mathematics formed no part of the System, tho' we could find instructors unconnected with the School. For French I sought the aid of Monsieur Miette, one of the French Refugee Congregation. For Mathematics I enjoyed the instruction of that benevolent man Rev. Henry Hutchesson . . . .' Gilbert's claim must be balanced against the references in James Six's letters, quoted above, to algebra and Euclid. Perhaps under Naylor the curriculum had actually narrowed.

One of Gilbert's companions for mathematical tuition, William Broughton, became the first Bishop of Australia. There he founded the colony's oldest school, The King's School, Parramatta, 'named after my own'. He gives his own name today to Broughton House. The other, Charles Plater, proposed the foundation of Marlborough College to provide affordable education for clergymen's sons.

Naylor, Gilbert writes, was 'a dignified looking man but with much severity of aspect and disposition. . . . The rod was his great dependence on all boys but those in first class . . . I respected him, but did not love him.' He once deprived the school of its usual week's holiday at Easter, a punishment the boys considered to be undeserved. 'Headed therefore by Johnny Gregory – then first Monitor – we went in a body to the Vice Dean Dr Welfit and begged his interference. The Doctor came down in the afternoon to the School and so effectual was his intercession, that Naylor promised to give the Holiday for the next week, if we were diligent that week. This was gratefully accepted, for that Easter-tide was stormy and unfit for out-door occupations.'

For John Francis, lower master, Gilbert had warmer feelings. 'He was very kind to me and gave me valuable advice when I had come to the head of the school. I shall never forget his kindness in this respect.' Though Francis was liked by Gilbert, he was not always tactful. Writing to the guardian of the two Medhurst boys who arrived at the school a couple of years before Gilbert, he says 'with regard to the abilities of the two young men, neither of them most certainly are of the first rate'. He goes on to compare them unfavourably to another boy: 'As to young Elwyn, few were endued with such ability. He certainly was a first rate genius, and would have done great credit to the King's School, had the Almighty been pleased to spare his life.'

The school's tradition of play-acting was maintained in Gilbert's time. 'The King's Scholars always bespoke a play', he writes, 'and begged their friends and others to take tickets. It was considered good fun to go round to the ladies schools to solicit their patronage, especially to one old puritan lady, a Miss Drake who wore a large Turban, and dismissed the applicants severely.' But the school's plays no longer had any connection with Speech Days.

These now occurred twice instead of four times a year, the first on Ascension Day, the second to coincide with the School Feast Day some time in September. On Ascension Day three senior boys made Latin or Greek speeches before the Dean and three or four prebendaries, who rewarded them by asking for a school holiday to last until afternoon service the following Saturday. James Six's reaction when given the Greek speech, and other references to these speeches in letters to Tylden, show what an honour it was to be chosen to speak.

On the School Feast day there was usually just one speech, made by the senior boy 'composed (as supposed) by the Master'. But when the Feast Society celebrated what it considered to be its centenary (1818 – see page 42) there must have been others, for Gilbert reports that 'Lord Tenterden [Charles Abbott] was so overpowered that he could not make a speech but amid floods of tears could only say "I thank you, I thank you, I am unable to speak" '. The wig-maker's son clearly retained as warm an affection for his old school as did Gilbert.

The same cannot be said about George Trimnell, who probably arrived at the school about three years after Gilbert. In his memoirs (passages from which were first published in 1956) he assembles all the ill he can say of it. Two things lie behind his bitterness: he was, he admits, a dull boy, and suffered for it; and he later became an earnest Nonconformist.

His most surprising comment on the curriculum is that 'no Scripture was read, nor was any religious instruction whatever given excepting once in four years when a Confirmation was about to take place in the Cathedral'. His most serious criticism of the teaching is that such subjects as were taught in theory, in fact weren't taught, but were left for the boys to learn on their own. A notice on the outside of the schoolroom door read *Aut disce, aut discede* (either learn or leave). On the inside of the door, he says, there should have been a notice reading *Aut* doce, *aut discede* (either *teach* or leave).

It was simpler for the masters, he claims, to chastise than teach. 'I got a large share of the former, being sometimes flogged two or three times a day, and perhaps also not allowed to go home to get my breakfast or dinner. And I think I have sometimes been kept in the School the whole day, from six to seven in the morning till six in the evening, and being locked up when the School hours were finished and remaining a prisoner till my mother wrote a note and sent my sister Mary to beg that I might be released.'

As a result he would sometimes play truant for two weeks at a time, arguing that 'If I go to school I am certain of almost daily punishment, and if I stay away for a time I can but be flogged when I return'. But this gave him little relief. 'I was very miserable from the fear of detection, and I knew not where to go. Three times every day I had to wander about where I thought I was least likely to be seen or met by any of my relatives; for I had many in Canterbury who, if they should meet me anywhere in school hours would make such enquiries as would lead to my detection.'

After a year as a commoner, he was examined by the Dean and Chapter for his scholarship. Fortunately they were keen to admit him because the numbers of scholars had fallen to about twenty. He returned from the examination much relieved that he had not been branded by the verger 'on the soft part' of his 'posterior', as other scholars had told him he would be, but was subjected to a ceremonial 'buffeting' after each of the three first occasions on which he wore his surplice in the cathedral. Back in the schoolroom, the older boys, 'having taken off their surplices, holding them by the skirt . . . form a circle, and . . . one of the younger boys, who has lately been admitted, is allowed, or rather compelled, to rush into the circle with his surplice on, which he is required to take off, and put into a bag suspended round his neck, whilst the boys of the circle are buffeting him with all their might. It frequently happens that when the poor little urchin has almost succeeded in bagging his surplice and only a corner remains out, one of his persecutors will seize the corner and pull a good part of the surplice out again.'

The final verdict on Naylor must be severe. Though Gilbert says he was a good scholar, he seems to have been an idle teacher and a severe flogger. And, as Trimnell confirms, there was a dramatic decline in the school's numbers, so that when he died in 1816 there were only 18 scholars and 8 commoners. The Napoleonic Wars were in part responsible. Other schools suffered similar declines in these years. But the decline at the King's School was also a consequence of a decision taken by the Dean and Chapter in 1785, the year they appointed Naylor. As one way of increasing the salaries of the two masters they ordered that monies which became available because scholarships were vacant should become the masters'. Naylor therefore had a financial interest in reducing the number of his scholars, as he effectively did.

The Revd John Birt, who succeeded Naylor, came with warm recommendations from, among others, the Bishop and Dean of Hereford, where he had been a priest-vicar at the cathedral. Numbers at the school quickly rose to 70, but Birt was

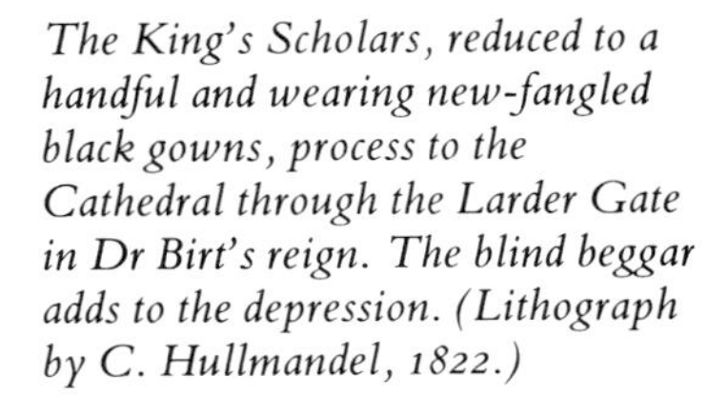

The King's Scholars, reduced to a handful and wearing new-fangled black gowns, process to the Cathedral through the Larder Gate in Dr Birt's reign. The blind beggar adds to the depression. (Lithograph by C. Hullmandel, 1822.)

a better musician than scholar, and was presently in trouble with the Dean and Chapter. In December 1829 they sent examiners to the school who reported badly of the top class and worse of the fourth and fifth classes, taught by the Revd William Jones, lower master. 'The boys really know nothing. Several of them, who had been three years in the school, could not decline a noun substantive nor had they an idea of syntax or of construing the easiest Latin Book. We expressed strongly to Mr Jones our opinion of the disgraceful state of this part of the school.' Jones resigned, and by 1832 numbers, which had sunk to about 40, had risen again to 60.

During his time Birt introduced 'black cloth gowns, breeches and caps' for scholars, replacing the 'purple stuff gowns' they had previously worn in Lent, on Speech Days, and when the archbishop was in residence, with the intention, according to Gilbert, of flattering Dean Andrews, 'who had been of Westminster School'. Possibly the change explains Woodruff and Cape's otherwise unexplained report that the school under Birt once broke into open revolt. There are other examples of the boys of the King's School resenting the introduction of foreign customs and Woodruff could have heard of it from his father who had been a boy under Birt.

Birt had private as well as professional problems, the principal of which was the elopement of his young wife. He has generally been seen as the model for Dr Strong, headmaster of the school which Dickens' David Copperfield attends at Canterbury, who is similarly deserted; Dickens denied that he modelled Strong on Birt, but the coincidences in their stories make it seem likely that he did. Strong, as Dickens describes him, is likeable but bumbling – 'almost as rusty as the tall iron rails and gates outside the house . . .'. His clothes are 'not particularly well brushed, and his hair not particularly well combed; his knee-smalls unbraced; his long black gaiters unbuttoned; and his shoes yawning like two caverns on the hearth-rug'. But he is 'the idol of the whole school'.

When Birt resigned it was exactly 50 years since the school had had a headmaster who was an unqualified success. Now at last the Dean and Chapter chose well. George Wallace would often tell the story of his arrival at Canterbury. As a young man just down from Cambridge he was recommended by his father to take advice about his future from his old headmaster at Charterhouse, Dr Russell, now a prebendary at Canterbury and Rector of St Botolph's, Bishopsgate. Standing on the rectory doorstep with the knocker in his hand, Wallace suddenly decided that he hadn't the courage to speak to Russell, and was about to turn away when he lost his hold and it fell with a clang. Instantly Russell opened the door and called him in. Russell suggested that he should apply for the position of lower master at the King's School, and this was what he had been for 18 months when the Dean and Chapter promoted him to headmaster.

Wallace was not only young for the job but neither an MA nor in holy orders. 'Both difficulties . . . were satisfactorily solved', Woodruff and Cape write, and suggest that it was Dr Russell who persuaded the archbishop to ordain him and grant him a Lambeth degree (Wallace put matters right by getting a Cambridge degree four years later).

During the next 27 years Wallace 'ruled by love not fear'; he had undertaken never to use corporal punishment and would send boys instead to the Dean or

Gad's Hill Place,
Higham by Rochester, Kent.

Saturday Twenty Fourth November 1865

Dear Sir

In thanking you for your obliging letter and its accompanying little book, allow me to assure you that I never was at the King's School, Canterbury; and that if there be any resemblance between David Copperfield's Doctor Strong and the Doctor Birt whom you mention, it must be purely accidental, inasmuch as I never before heard of the existence of the last-named gentleman.

Dear Sir
Faithfully Yours
Charles Dickens

The Rev: J. S. Sidebotham

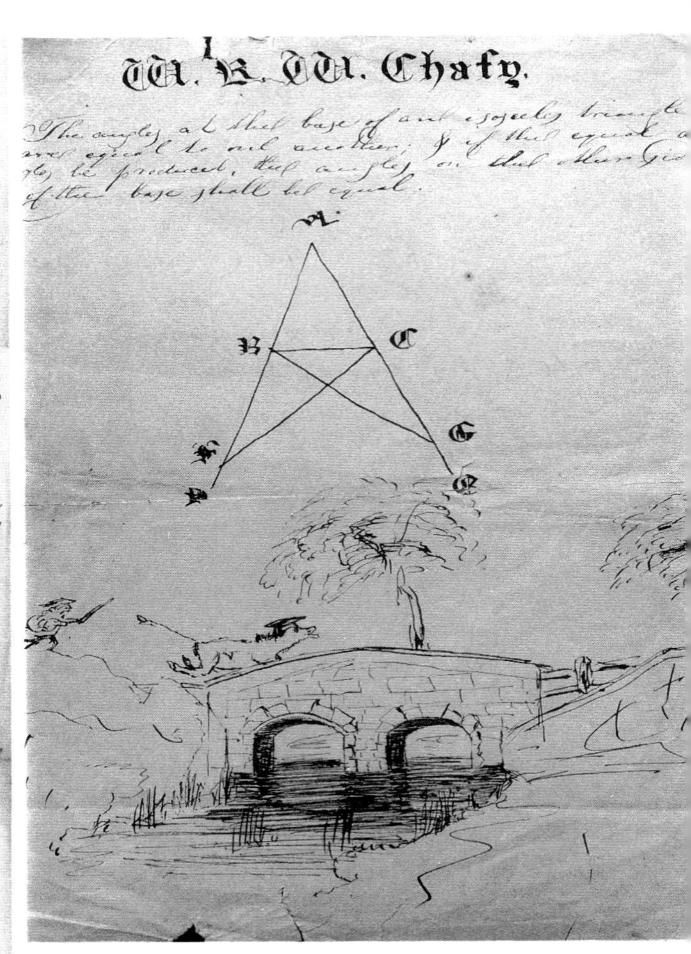

Under George Wallace the curriculum expanded. To prove Euclid's 'Asses' Bridge' Proposition proved beyond W. K. W. Chafy in the examinations of 1856.

Charles Dickens denied in this letter to J. S. Sidebotham, compiler of the Memorials of the King's School *(1865), that he had based David Copperfield's headmaster Dr Strong on Dr Birt of King's. The parallels are striking, nevertheless.*

Vice-dean for a supposedly alarming reprimand. One boy, sitting with bowed head at the Dean's mahogany table, was less alarmed than he should have been and managed to carve his name, Arthur M..., on its fine surface while Archdeacon Croft lectured him. He was expelled.

Wallace made serious attempts to widen the school's curriculum, introducing the regular teaching of mathematics, and appointing a French master. M. Martinet of the University of Paris held this post for 30 years. Another Frenchman recruited by Wallace was the artist L. L. Razé, whose illustrations of the school give such a clear impression of its buildings and ceremonials in the 1840s and 50s. Razé had arrived in Canterbury at the age of nineteen on his way to London to try to sell his work to publishers there, but had been so impressed by the cathedral's beauty that he stayed for the rest of his life. He was the school's drawing master from 1824 to 1865.

Meanwhile, in 1856 Wallace had divided the upper forms of the school into two departments. Boys leaving the fourth form could now transfer to the Special Department where they would study such subjects as surveying, military drawing, and fortifications (of which Razé described himself as 'professor'). As well as the

The Schoolroom in the Almonry was drawn by a boy, James Wallace, in about 1843. After nearly three centuries of use it was demolished in the 1860s rebuilding undertaken by Dr Mitchinson.

usual modern languages they could learn, from the German master, Sanscrit, Hindustani, and Persian. This master was Dr Röst, a scholar of some standing at St Augustine's, not the typical King's School master of the time. These were the great days of the British Empire, and the Special Department was clearly meant to train soldiers and imperial administrators, but Wallace's attempt to found something like an 'army class' was premature, and did not last beyond his time.

Wallace increased the school's numbers so successfully that by 1848, when there were in total about 90 boys, he applied to the Dean and Chapter for permission to raise funds for a new schoolroom. The Dean and Chapter did not object, though at first they only offered him 'any old timber or materials at our disposal'. Next year they were more generous, and by 1855 the School Feast Society was able to report that the completion of a second schoolroom was due solely to the liberality of the Dean and Chapter. 'Your committee can now point with satisfaction to the School buildings, which are at once most convenient for use and highly ornamental to the City of Canterbury.' The new schoolroom was designed by the old King's Scholar, Harry Austin, surveyor and architect to the Dean and Chapter, and is shown in one of Razé's sketches, built above the Norman arches immediately to the south of the Norman Staircase (see endpapers). The Norman style is so well copied that it deceived the 1990 (draft) Michelin Guide. The space between these arches had previously been known as 'The Little Mint Yard'. What Razé's sketch does not show is that at one corner of The Little Mint Yard lived 'Mrs Norton, a lady of great celebrity', who sold tarts, buns, etc., to the boys of the school, and that near her house she kept a number of pigs; one by one these would become her pies and sausages. In 1936 the new schoolroom became the school library and remained so till 1990 when the library moved to Butterfield's splendid building at St Augustine's.

In 1834 Wallace was almost involved in a more imaginative extension of the school: the acquisition of the ruins of St Augustine's. It was probably he (since it was not the Dean and Chapter) who took legal advice which at first favoured the idea but later concluded that it was not possible because the property belonged to a lunatic and an Act of Parliament would be required before it could be sold.

'The Gentlemen of the King's School', joint dedicatees of this c. 1845 lithograph by their drawing master, L. L. Razé, idle and buy tuck by the Green Court Gate.

The post-Reformation history of this great monastery – founded and dedicated to St Peter and St Paul by the saint soon after his arrival in England in 597, renamed St Augustine's by St Dunstan in 978, dissolved in 1538 – had been complex. Henry VIII had demolished the monks' quarters and the church, making the remainder into 'the King's House'. Queen Elizabeth gave it to Lord Cobham – but stayed there on her visit to Canterbury in 1573. It next passed to the Wotton and then the Hales families, the second of whom pillaged it for materials for their mansion, Hales Place (above the school's playing field known as Birley's). Thereafter various owners bought various pieces of what remained of the buildings and grounds, and by 1830 it was part brewery, part amusement park. 'The gardens adjoining the resting place of nuns and monks', writes the author of *The Autobiography of a Man of Kent*, 'were used as a bowling-green and tea-drinking place for the plebeians of Canterbury.' He has had, he adds, 'many a draught . . . of the good home-brewed beverage manufactured under its sacred roof. A part of the original building was used as a fives-court . . . I have seen some good matches played there . . . . Fireworks, balloons, and the Blondin of those days attracted crowds of Canterbury lads and lasses'.

The advice which persuaded Wallace to abandon the idea of buying the abbey proved correct. Three Acts of Parliament were required before it could be sold. It was William Broughton, Bishop of Australia, who then accidentally influenced its future. From Australia he wrote to his English friend Edward Coleridge, 'Pray do your best to bring about . . . the design of a seminary in which students may be trained for the sacred office in the Colonies'. Coleridge went to A. J. Beresford Hope, the abbey's new owner, and told him what was needed. Beresford Hope, a wealthy man who apparently had no idea what to do with his new property, told Coleridge, 'St Augustine's is yours'. After Butterfield's extensive rebuilding the abbey was re-opened in 1848 as the Missionary College of St Augustine.

It is appropriate to mention the school's Feast Society again during Wallace's time, not only because he was its keen supporter, but because its activities reached a climax in these years. As Gilbert remembered, its Feast Day now coincided with one of the school's Speech Days. By 1840 the 'speeches' on this day had been transferred from the schoolroom to the Chapter House, and the programme for 1844 shows how elaborate they had become. The boys delivered, presumably from memory, 19 different monologues or dialogues from Roman, Greek, French, and modern English writers, starting with Milton and ending with Terence. The members of the society then dined at the Fountain Hotel, listened to after-dinner speeches, and drank numerous toasts before returning to the schoolroom for a concert and dance. The events of the day lasted 15 hours without a break.

During the previous century and a quarter the monies raised by the society to support scholars at the universities had steadily increased. At first about £50 a year was collected each Feast Day, but later two exhibitions were supported with sums of between £40 and £50 a year. Two King's Scholars who benefited have been mentioned: Sir Egerton Brydges and Charles Abbott. From 1829 two formal exhibitions of £60 each were supported by the society. It was not until five years after Wallace retired that it abandoned its original name and became more decorously known as the King's School Exhibition Fund Society.

In his reminiscences, *I Remember*, the Revd John W. Horsley describes curious features of the school in Wallace's time. 'In the lower half of the school marbles were not yet considered below the dignity of a public school; they had their definite season, and were played in various ways which required skill or were merely governed by chance. Another weird occupation was the making of "togey", a delight quite unintelligible to me now, as it had not even the advantage of being a forbidden pursuit. We got a chunk of indiarubber, softened it somewhat by stabs from a penknife, and then laboriously chewed it day after day, until it became so plastic that, doubling it over, we enclosed a bubble of air which could be made to explode with a mild pop.'

'Dr Wallace', Horsley writes, 'was a gentleman and a scholar of the old type – burly, bellowing, and benevolent, a lovable teacher and an inveterate punster.' Well-loved as he was, Wallace had weaknesses. If given the chance he would preach sermons or make speeches of phenomenal length. One in the cathedral lasted an hour and a quarter; an afternoon address to the Canterbury Farmers' Club lasted over an hour and contained 'quotation after quotation from the classics, bearing upon the subject of agriculture'. He was also roused to untypical fury by any form of water sport, and once gave a boy a whole book of Homer to write out for swimming in the Stour.

In his later years he often left the school to manage itself and retired to his rented house, Heppington Hall, three miles outside Canterbury in the village of Lower Hardres. But the school did not suffer unduly, and the feelings for him which those he taught retained for the rest of their lives were of affection and gratitude.

Best known of Wallace's pupils was Walter Pater, whose elegant prose writings were once so admired, and who is again much studied as an aesthetics philosopher, especially in the USA and Japan, though his reputation was tainted when Oscar Wilde named him in court as an influence. About Pater, Wallace had already had reservations. In his farewell speech he hoped that God would preserve Pater 'as a faithful member of that Church in whose principles you have been strictly brought up'. 'I cannot say', Wallace continued, 'that you have been an active monitor in suppressing turbulence and punishing the refractory', but he concluded that Pater might have qualities which in future would redound to his own credit and to the honour of the school.

Pater's homosexual inclinations are clear enough. He had the classic circumstance of losing his father when he was only two. For years he lived as a bachelor Oxford don, then for the rest of his life with his two sisters. Furthermore, as his university friend, Ingram Bywater, euphemistically puts it, 'You will notice, I think [in Pater's writings] a certain sympathy with a certain aspect of Greek life'. But there is no suggestion of homosexuality about Pater's relationships with his two closest friends at school: John Rainer McQueen and Henry Dombrain. Together the three boys formed what they called the Triumvirate. Together they took part in the great snowball fight, the snowballs filled with stones, against the boys of the town, which oddly enough so exhilarated Pater. Together they performed on Speech Days. Both later betrayed Pater, Dombrain by becoming a narrowly High Church clergyman, McQueen by intervening to prevent Pater's ordination.

The boy he *was* probably in love with was Joseph Haydock. When asked what animal Haydock suggested to him, Pater replied, 'A handsome ferocious young bull'. Haydock did not respond, but some 35 years later he was to be the model for James Stokes in Pater's long short story, *Emerald Uthwart*. Emerald, a young man to whom Pater gives many of his own feelings about the school, forms a romantic alliance with Stokes; together they go to the wars, but there they disobey orders and undertake the private capture of an enemy flag. For this Stokes is executed, and though Emerald is reprieved, he returns home disgraced, sickens, and dies. Only too late is he forgiven and sent back his commission.

Pater wrote *Emerald Uthwart* after a moving return to Canterbury in 1891. He makes no attempt to disguise the school. Dark Entry, Green Court, and Cathedral are all named. So is that King's School tradition of the time, the paper-chase. Emerald (unlike Pater who was not athletic) 'loves best . . . to run a paper-chase afar over the marshes, till you come in sight, or within scent of the sea, in the autumn twilight; and his dutifulness to games at least had its reward. A wonderful hit of his at cricket was long remembered; right over the lime-trees on to the cathedral roof, was it? or over the roof, and onward into space, circling there independently, minutely, as *Sidus Cantiorum*? . . .'.

8

MITCHINSON – REFORM WITH TEARS

THE DEAN AND CHAPTER CHOSE AS WALLACE'S SUCCESSOR, WITHOUT CONSIDERING ANY OTHER CANDIDATE, A YOUNG MAN OF 25 WHO HAD HAD JUST TWO YEARS' TEACHING experience. Risky as this might seem, especially when they were concerned about the school's decline in the last years of Wallace's amiable but lax regime, events proved that they knew what they were doing. Instantly the Revd John Mitchinson set about reform and within 14 years he had transformed the school.

He came originally from Durham, where his mother (whom be brought with him to Canterbury) had run a girls' school, after his father, a merchant seaman, had died probably without ever seeing the child. A fatherless boy, at Durham School he had made its headmaster, Edward Elder, his hero. 'Elder', he writes, was 'one of those ideal schoolmasters who are only produced once or twice in a generation'. So it was to be expected that Mitchinson, after getting a double first at Pembroke College, Oxford, should become a teacher himself. He went to the Merchant Taylors' School, and it was from there, two years later, that Canon Stanley (later Dean of Westminster) brought him to Canterbury.

Dr Mitchinson with pupils: the photograph is undated but belongs to the earlier years of his headmastership.

Today Mitchinson seems such a classic example of the Victorian flogging headmaster that the great benefits he brought the school are easily overlooked. Fortunately these were fully described by his next-but-one successor, Thomas Field, as well as trenchantly by himself. Field had reason for admiring Mitchinson; Mitchinson had picked him out while examining at Faversham Grammar School and brought him to the King's School, where at the age of fourteen he had become head boy.

Mitchinson felt no such loyalty to Wallace. 'When I went down to see the K.S.C.', he writes, 'I can tell you my heart sank within me. Anything more inconceivably squalid can hardly be imagined. . . . Wallace had contented himself with a day school, the numbers of which had sunk to between fifty and sixty. . . . The scholarship fund was practically wasted in paying the greater part of their fees. He endeavoured to advertise the school by elaborate prize-givings, held in the Chapter House. . . . But in spite of all his efforts, the entrance diminished.'

The school's decline was only in part Wallace's fault. By 1860 Canterbury had become something of a provincial backwater, and its more enterprising citizens were being drawn away to growing cities like Birmingham. Furthermore, over the previous 20 years, railways had transformed travel in England making it easy

The celebration of Speeches, at one time in the Schoolroom but moved by Wallace to the splendour of the Chapter House, was considered rather useless by the pragmatic Mitchinson; but he kept it on. (Lithograph by L. L. Razé, 1845.)

for the middle classes to send their sons to distant schools. Though Kentish families did not on the whole choose the new schools – Cheltenham, Haileybury, etc. – which were founded all over the country from 1840 onwards, they *did* increasingly send their sons to the great public schools, in particular Eton, Harrow, and Westminster. In Kent itself there was already more competition and more to come. St Edmund's School had moved to Canterbury in 1855, Dover College was to be founded in 1871, and St Lawrence College, Ramsgate, in 1879, while Tonbridge, considered a particular rival, had had a reforming headmaster since 1843. It was

Mitchinson who understood how the King's School was becoming threatened by competition, and how it was prevented from competing successfully because of its circumscribed space. It was he who, above all by a great building programme, made it into a national public school.

The school in theory had sleeping space for 20 or 30 boarders in the old school house, once the Almonry, as well as for others in the headmaster's house, the lower master's house, the organist's house, and in certain dames' houses in the city. But according to Mitchinson, when he first visited Canterbury there were in fact only 12 boarders. In any case there was too little boarding space for the school he planned. His most important expansion to provide for this was the building of a new headmaster's house and school house on the east and north sides of the Mint Yard, respectively, to accommodate 60 boarders.

Towards it the Dean and Chapter contributed £6000–7000. 'But with that their liberality ceased', Mitchinson writes in his delightfully frank autobiographical fragment. 'Old Stone, the treasurer, had a reputation for stinginess founded on a sour wrinkled face. But he was no worse than the others: stately Dean Alford, "Tubby" Robertson, the courtly Bishop of Dover, or Archdeacon Harrison, except that he held the bag and therefore had the disagreeable duty of saying no. The Chapter felt that we had had enough. As Robertson once said to me "You know, Headmaster, we do not wish the Cathedral to exist as an appanage to the King's School".'

The dormitories of the new School House were divided into cubicles, an important change. The cubicle system, Field writes, did 'more than is generally supposed to abolish some barbarous and pagan features of public school life. . . . One whose

W. A. Boone succeeded L. L. Razé as drawing master in 1865. With this lithograph of the 'New School House' (now Galpin's) built by Mitchinson he made a good début.

Boys' cubicles were introduced by Mitchinson, following Edward Thring, in the mid-1860s. The young servant who emptied the slops was ex officio called Pots.

school life began some eighteen months after the change can testify that whatever traces of roughness remained, there was a thoroughly sound tradition in all moral matters.' Mitchinson based his cubicles on those he saw at Uppingham, where he had gone to learn from its famous headmaster, Edward Thring. His relationship with Thring was ambiguous. To Mitchinson, Thring wrote, 'You are the only honest man I ever met in the profession, you came and picked my brains, but you have openly and freely at all times acknowledged the obligation'. About Thring, Mitchinson writes, 'When he talked, and he talked much, one seemed to hear the preface "Thus saith the Lord" '. And about the visiting sermon Thring preached at Canterbury, 'As far as I was concerned the sermon consisted of a series of short barks, which were to me entirely unintelligible . . . but . . . I liked him much, for he was a good fellow and his general bonhomie helped to disperse the vapours which his teaching sometimes created'.

To expand further the school's premises, Mitchinson at first planned to rebuild the old Almonry, but this was unfortunately considered impossible and it was demolished. As a result the Mint Yard was thrown open to the roadway which led from the town to the Green Court. But across this road stood the Grange, built by George Austin, Harry Austin's father, in mediaeval style in about 1840. The school now obtained possession of this and built on to its west end rooms for more boys. Others were boarded in a building which faced the Green Court and, because it was the house of Mr Hodgson, the mathematics master, became known as Hodgson's Hall. By the time Mitchinson left in 1873 his building programme had enabled him to raise the school's numbers to 137.

Even before his rebuilding, he had transformed the school's 50 scholarships. Twenty-five probationers were now to be supported for two years by the same stipends as before (£10 16*s* 8*d*). They might then be promoted to one of fifteen Junior Scholarships, supported by a full remission of school fees (£15 15*s*). After three years Junior Scholars could be elected to one of ten Senior Scholarships with a value of £30 each which they might hold for another two years. These changes had the same purpose. The probationers could be day boys but the scholarships, especially the senior ones, would be large enough to attract boarders. 'And in a very short time [they] did so', Mitchinson writes.

The arrangements for examination and election of scholars continued, however, to be curiously primitive. The boys would stand in line and a member of the Chapter would ask them geography, history, and general knowledge questions. A boy who answered correctly would keep his place, or, if any boy or boys above him had failed to answer, would be moved up the line to stand above them. When the examination ended those who stood highest in the line were elected. 'I can still recall', Field writes, 'the pain and anxiety of losing some places and the triumph of recovery with an answer about the Alleghany Mountains.' One of his friends claimed to have lost his scholarship 'solely because he refused to believe there was a town in New Zealand called Canterbury'. 'As the youngest boy', J. W. Horsley writes about his own election as a King's Scholar, 'I stood at the bottom of a row, but the question having been passed down, "What is the English of *radix*?" I alone could answer it. So I marched up to the top. There I was asked, "What is its dative plural?" Triumphantly, having been taught Latin by my mother, I answered, "*Radicibus*". This was all. This was enough. I passed, and went back into the great schoolroom to the astonishment of the boys there, who saw the youngest come out first.'

Even 'at the close of the Seventies', R. A. Bosanquet remembers that 'in place of an Oxford Examiner [who would come a few years later] with black bag and umbrella, was an array of eminent churchmen, in the full fig of their doctor's robes.... Perhaps these distinguished scholars were a trifle rusty in the more elementary parts of their scholarship: at any rate they ... made the viva voce so elementary that, if we could have understood the questions, every boy would, I think, have come out equal first. But here not seldom the light failed ...

'Canon X: "P o'o'llbo."

'No answer.

'Canon X (to next boy): "P o'o'llbo."

'No answer ...

'Canon X (very loudly): "P o'o'o'llbo."

'The boy: "I beg your pardon, Sir?" ...

'As a different type I will take Canon Y ... who would have loved to dispense scholarships all round lest any should be disappointed ...

'Canon Y: "Now, my lad, can you tell me *who* won this battle?"

'Youth: "Oh – er – the *Greeks*, Sir."

'Canon: "Well, well! Now I am *sure* you know better than that. Think again, think again!"

'Youth: "The *Romans* then, Sir."

'Canon: "Very good! But why didn't you say so at *first* if you knew it! ... The Romans – quite right." '

Today the most modern of Mitchinson's teaching practices would seem to be his refusal to allow early specialization. 'Cram of every kind was abhorent to the headmaster's mind .... There was no ... boiling down of history and general knowledge into the form of methodical answers to such questions as experience suggested a judicious examiner might be likely to propound ....' Mathematics and modern languages were now regular parts of the curriculum, and so in a small way was science. Mitchinson was the first headmaster of any school to have a science as well as a classical degree, and he turned part of Hodgson's Hall, described as 'a sort of scullery at the back', into a laboratory for chemistry teaching. The Dean and Chapter made a somewhat modest contribution: £4 for an air pump. Ironically, in 1871, it was as a memorial to the dean that funds raised by a national subscription were used to build the Alford Laboratory in the Mint Yard. Mitchinson even started a school museum 'in a damp cupboard of the classroom under the arches'.

Alongside so much that seems modern, it was odd that he should maintain one exaggerated feature of the traditional teaching of classics: the learning by heart of Horace. If Walter Pater was not inventing, this had long been a school tradition. 'Horace', he wrote: 'he was, had been always, the idol of their school; to know him by heart, to translate him into effective English idiom, have an apt phrase of his instinctively on one's lips for every occasion. That boys should be made to spout him under penalties, would have seemed doubtless to that sensitive, vain, winsome poet ... quite the sorriest of fates; might have seemed not so bad however, could he ... have peeped on these English boys, row upon row, with black or golden heads, repeating him in the fresh morning, and observed how well for once the thing was done.' Reciting Horace was also a Durham tradition and this may have been one reason for Mitchinson continuing to enforce the rule that no boy could enter the sixth form until he had learned by heart all four books of the Odes.

Mitchinson's influence extended beyond the school, for it was his initiative which led to the founding of the Headmasters' Conference. In 1869, when Parliament was discussing a bill which would establish a commission to regulate the smaller 'endowed schools' of the country (it had regulated the nine major public schools the year before) Mitchinson invited 'a considerable number of my brother Headmasters' to meet at the Freemasons' Tavern in London. The meeting sent a deputation to discuss the bill with the minister responsible for education. When the headmasters met again at Uppingham Thring became their leader and the formal founder of the Conference. 'If I may claim to have laid the egg,' Mitchinson writes, 'Thring did all the clucking necessary.'

Mitchinson's (and Thring's) fears were that the planned Commission would exercise an unwanted bureaucratic control over schools like theirs and that as a result they would be 'tied to the chariot wheels of the Great Schools'. The Headmasters' Conference failed to prevent the establishment of the Commission, but was probably responsible for it proving helpful rather than restrictive.

Boys who were not terrified of Mitchinson remembered him as the most inspiring of teachers, continuously keen to interest them in every aspect of the world around them. On Saturday evenings he would read to them from Trollope or Tennyson, or from the newly published *Alice through the Looking-Glass*. 'I cannot think what you see in that book,' said Dean Alford. 'It has no moral.' 'Just why

PLATE 9
Top: Bailey, the girls' house at St Augustine's, is an 18th and 19th-century 'conversion' of the Abbey's cemetery gate. The Roman road from the coast which here makes a kink to bypass the ancient burial ground must have seen many traffic hold-ups of the sort shown in this Paul Sandby aquatint (1782).

Bottom: The main quadrangle at St Augustine's as it was when St Augustine's College opened in 1848 after the magnificent restoration and extension of the Abbey buildings by William Butterfield. L. L. Razé who made this lithograph was drawing master at the King's School for some forty years. The central building is now the School Library and on the left is Tradescant House.

CEMETERY GATE OF St AUGUSTINES MONASTERY AT CANTERBURY.

PLATE 10 The Green Court with the King's Scholars processing towards the Cathedral through the Larder Gate, under the 149-year old lime trees. When Dean Alford built the Dean's Steps the Scholars took to their present route. Water-colour by William Burgess, 1857.

I like it,' Mitchinson replied. Across the marshes round the city he would take paper chases. These usually led, according to Horsley, 'to Grove Ferry, over, into, or through some thirty or forty ditches (locally called dykes), ending with a swim in the Stour with our clothes on to get off the mud of the dykes, then a game of bowls at the Ferry hostelry'. 'Who can forget', Field writes, 'that splendid climax of shandy-gaff, cheese and biscuits, the like of which the world has ceased to produce, or the subsequent march back to Canterbury along the road to the accompaniment of . . . songs of the American Civil War.'

On the other hand, country walks with the headmaster (always accompanied by his Pomeranian, Fritz) would sometimes be 'treats for the boys who came to him for voluntary preparation at some unearthly hour in the morning'. And Edward Rendall, another great admirer, admits that beneath the surface of Mitchinson's botanizing walks 'there ran a thread of bitterness. He never realised that chastisement was no joke to us, and often allowed himself a strain of humorous banter, which, seeing that it often meant trouble on the morrow, sometimes spoiled our enjoyment.' Field admits that 'There can be few periods in the history of any school where the wits of every single boy received more salutary sharpening and the energies of every idler more individual awakening . . . .'

The parents of one boy who had received some individual awakening charged Mitchinson with assault. 'The cause was laughed out of court', Mitchinson writes. He describes how the boys of the sixth form had a fly waiting for him outside the Guildhall, where the case was heard, and when he was acquitted took the horses out and 'dragged me back in triumph to the school. The fuss which the case caused did me more good than harm.' When he applied for the headmastership of Charterhouse, a job he did not get, he was told that the boys there had favoured him. The *Kentish Gazette*'s long report of the case adds details. The victim's story was that Mitchinson had attacked him for mistakes in a Greek lesson, hitting him across the chest, back, and shoulders with a cane twenty or twenty-five times – doctors described his injuries. And though the paper confirms that the boys of the school cheered Mitchinson and dragged him home in a fly, it notes that a large crowd of townspeople hissed him.

Eventually at the King's School there was rebellion. Mitchinson's apparently frank account of this claims that it began with 'a piece of insubordinate rudeness' by a boy, 'C', to a monitor, Kearney. When Kearney next morning licked 'C', several days of anti-monitor rioting followed, in which Mitchinson did not intervene, until he heard that the boys had been singing the Marseillaise and provisioning the hall (their dayroom) against a siege.

Then, to simplify, he ordered the expulsion of four ringleaders and the flogging of thirty more, seven each day during the following week. The first seven had been flogged when Mitchinson received confirmation of his appointment as Bishop of Barbados, and made this the reason for declaring an amnesty.

When Mitchinson's account was eventually published (1933) in *The Cantuarian* it provoked a bitter answer from the Revd F. N. Crowther, one of the members of the rising. The revolt, according to Crowther 'was not a mere senseless outbreak . . . against necessary discipline, but a protest against a tyranny and brutality both in the school and out which a rising generation could no longer tolerate'. Though

When Mitchinson left King's the boys gave him an album with their photographs and below each he wrote the boy's name. Thomas Field and Francis Crowther carried into adult life strongly opposed views on the rebellion of 1873. The master above is C. W. Cobb, considered severe even by Mitchinson.

The monitors of 1873 in front of The Grange. Thomas Field, later Headmaster, is Captain of School.

the immediate provocation was the brutality of the monitors he did not blame them since they were only imitating their superiors, in particular Cobb, master of the Fourth Form, who 'had drawn up what he called a penal code, which made such simple mistakes as the infinitive for the subjunctive in a Latin prose subject to three hard blows on the cheek with his open hand: while three such faults in an exercise entitled a caning by the Hd.master'.

The boys, Crowther says, felt no bitterness against Mitchinson himself because he 'always allowed the culprit to make what defence he would'. 'But just imagine,' he adds, 'some 30 or more boys were to be caned but only at the rate of 7 a day, presumably because after inflicting over 40 strokes the Hd.master not only needed his luncheon – caning always took place at 12.45 p.m. – but also his arm required a rest.'

Birley, headmaster of the school in 1933, would not publish Crowther's letter in *The Cantuarian*, and Field, when shown it, wrote a long defence of Mitchinson. At the time of the revolt, although away at Oxford, Field had been head boy, and no doubt felt responsible for what Crowther saw as the monitors' brutal regime. But he confirmed that the school under Mitchinson was a rough place. When he first arrived there 'the bullying was brutal and continuous'. In the Forrens he saw one of the last of the formal fights which used to take place there. 'I have no idea what it was about, probably about nothing; for the School, at least the lower part of it, was arrayed in order of pugilistic prowess – so-and-so can lick so-and-so, and if there was any doubt about the point, it had to be decided. So in my first term it was discussed whether I could lick Hall or Hall could lick me. But the point did not interest us and we refused to engage in mortal combat for the amusement of others when we had no sort of quarrel with each other.'

Bishop Mitchinson in later life.

It should be added that the sadistic Mr Cobb moved to Uppingham, where Thring was delighted to have a 'Mitchinson man', and was well thought of there, though he remained unduly harsh.

Mitchinson departed to Barbados, a suitable place, a King's Scholar observed, because there 'canes grow wild and the boys wear no breeches'. From Barbados he wrote long (soon printed) letters to 'the Boys of the King's School', while enough remained who remembered him. His first ended, 'Mrs Mitchinson's forehead is well [she had been 'projected across the cabin' 'through a sudden lurch of the ship'], Miss Hole [his aunt] has stood the voyage excellently and is well, so is old Fritz.'

The final episode of Mitchinson's time at Canterbury should not obscure the fact that he was one of the great headmasters of the nineteenth century. The loyalty of his old pupils cannot be dismissed as merely that of sycophants; it included the respect of such a boy as Crowther, who in many ways disapproved of him. He seems a more sympathetic man if the philosophy which lay behind his behaviour is understood. He did not believe in the innocence of childhood, but considered there was 'much evil in actual operation in most boys' characters'. He *did* believe in the observance of law, and thought that this necesarily involved the punishment of those who broke it. His comments on the society of his time have an interestingly modern flavour. 'The great bane of our age is self-seeking: its motto is "Every man for himself". Selfishness tinges our entire national character . . . "How will it affect trade?" is the only criterion of right and wrong we ever affect to recognise in our international transactions . . . the conscience of the nation is measured by the price of stocks.'

On returning to England Mitchinson became Master of his old college, Pembroke; indeed his subsequent career was more distinguished than that of any other retired headmaster of the school. Tyrant or prophet – or something of both – there is little doubt that he did for the King's School in the nineteenth century what Shirley was to do for it in the twentieth; indeed but for its resurrection by Mitchinson there would probably have been no independent school for Shirley to rescue.

The whole School in Mitchinson's last year, 1873. He stands wearing his mortar-board below the dangling feet of the boy sitting in the lowest arch of the Norman Staircase, who is Thomas Field.

9
BLORE, FIELD AND GALPIN

'WITH THE ADVENT OF DR BLORE AND HIS CHARMING YOUNG WIFE', WRITES CROWTHER, 'AN ENTIRE CHANGE CAME OVER THE ATMOSPHERE OF THE SCHOOL, FOR which I for one was profoundly thankful, and my last two years there furnishes only happy memories.' The Revd W. G. Mosse, in his chapter for the 1908 history of the school, writes that his six years under Dr Blore were among the happiest of his life. 'No one could regard the Headmaster and Mrs Blore with greater admiration and love.' Others confirm that Blore's 13 years were as much of a contrast with Mitchinson's 14 years, as Mitchinson's years had been with Wallace's. 'Corporal punishment certainly had been administered with consistent severity', Moss continues. 'Under Dr Blore it was far less frequently resorted to .... Perhaps we began under this milder system dimly to entertain a higher sense of duty.'

Dr. Blore in the mid-1870s.

Reports of Blore's 'angelic qualities' had reached the school from his previous school at Bromsgrove. When, on the first Sunday after his arrival, there was a noticeable improvement in the menu, they seemed justified. According to Mosse, what the boys presently saw in his study also impressed them. Here Blore kept a special desk for the study of the New Testament, and on this the candles were frequently burnt to the sockets. 'Those burnt candles gave the doctor more influence than his best sermons.'

Blore's mildness did not prevent him from presiding over a sixth form with a workload and routine which today seems astonishing. 'The ordinary times of Preparation were ludicrously insufficient and, as we had an extra hour before breakfast already, there was nothing for it but to rise literally with the lark or even earlier. Not seldom I can remember being in my study by four o'clock a.m., and in summer pacing the Dark Entry, book in hand, long "before the early worm is up". Indeed, certain portions of the Classics are, in my mind, inseparably associated with memories of those lovely dewy mornings, the low sun casting strange shadows from the lime trees and among the ruins in the Cathedral gardens, and tingeing with rosy hues the soft grey stonework of the incomparable Bell Harry tower.'

Other memories of Mosse's capture a schoolboy's view of the outside world. 'Most of the Canons and Minor Canons seemed to have been always there, like the Cathedral. ... The courteous, silver-haired Canon Thomas; Canon Robertson, the Church historian, who for us was always "Tubby", with his peculiar trot as he passed us, humming, down the Dark Entry, stopping at intervals to call to his little terrier, "Come along, Jerry-Jeremiah!" or as he went (still humming and with the same peculiar trot) down the aisle to his stall in the Cathedral. The Venerable Benjamin Harrison, Archdeacon of Maidstone, who seemed always engaged during prayers in erasing marks in his big Prayer-book with his thumbnail.' These were the dean and canons whose examination methods were described earlier.

The tuck shop in the Norman arches under the Schoolroom (now the Memorial Chapel).

More closely connected with the school was Mother Obey, 'who kept the tuck shop at the porter's lodge, and was generally attended by her *enfant terrible* "Bobby". Her name will call up in the minds of many the wild rush in the "ten minutes" for buns and pies which were served us through the window, Mother Obey's recommendations on her wares being interspersed with tearful allusions to Obey's ill-treatment, and peevish exhortations to Bobby to keep his " 'ands off them tarts" '. And Billy Goodhew, the cricket coach, with 'his oft repeated cry of – "Play a bit more forrader, Sir!" or "Play a bit more lissomer" '. And Tommy Neaves, the bathman, with his 'never-varied raucous cry of "Now my little 'eroes" as he flung our towels to us over the wooden partition on bath nights'.

Mosse also had fond – or at least tolerant – memories of the masters of his time: of R. B. Gordon of the Fourth Form ('refined, aristocratic and scholarly'); of L. G. H. Mason of the Third Form for his help with dramatic 'entertainments of a lighter kind' which the boys occasionally performed, using the hall tables as a stage; and of the 'bearded and muscular' Revd Richard Hodgson. Hodgson was connected with an important school development. In September 1879 the Junior School was separated from the main school and he was made its first master. In an age of athletic heroes, a master who was himself a good bat, a fair fast bowler, and would play alongside the boys was guaranteed to be popular. It was Hodgson who had the Green Court returfed at his own expense – the turf remains the school's.

Billy Goodhew (far right) with the Cricket XI of 1888. Algernon Latter, future Headmaster, holds the bat.

Theatricals in the Grange garden, 1886. 'Tar' Mason, a celebrated producer of plays and Speeches, stands in the doorway.

In Blore's time the playing field which came to be known as Blore's was levelled so that cricket as well as football could be played there. Cricket of a sort had previously been played at least from Napoleonic War times in the Green Court, and as late as the 1860s football too. Here the opening match of the season, between boarders and day boys, resembled the game vividly described in *Tom Brown's Schooldays*. 'Of each side some twelve or so would do battle in the open, and all the rest were put in a serried phalanx in goal.' Even in the mid-1880s the school team was of no definite number; before a match with another school the two captains would agree about how large their sides should be. The Canterbury game had its own rules – a player, for example, could hold and run with the ball if chased, but as soon as the pursuit stopped he had to put it down; and the scoring was by 'games', each team collecting up to six or seven during a match. It was common for old King's Scholars and players from the city to take part, and matches were something of a Canterbury social occasion.

In Mitchinson's time (1862) the school football team had suffered a setback, recorded in the Football Club's accounts.

> 'On November 1st, in consequence of a rule that had been issued to the effect that only members of the Sixth Form should take the Football out, 11 boys . . . signed an insulting letter to the Sixth Form, and therein begged to resign their places as they

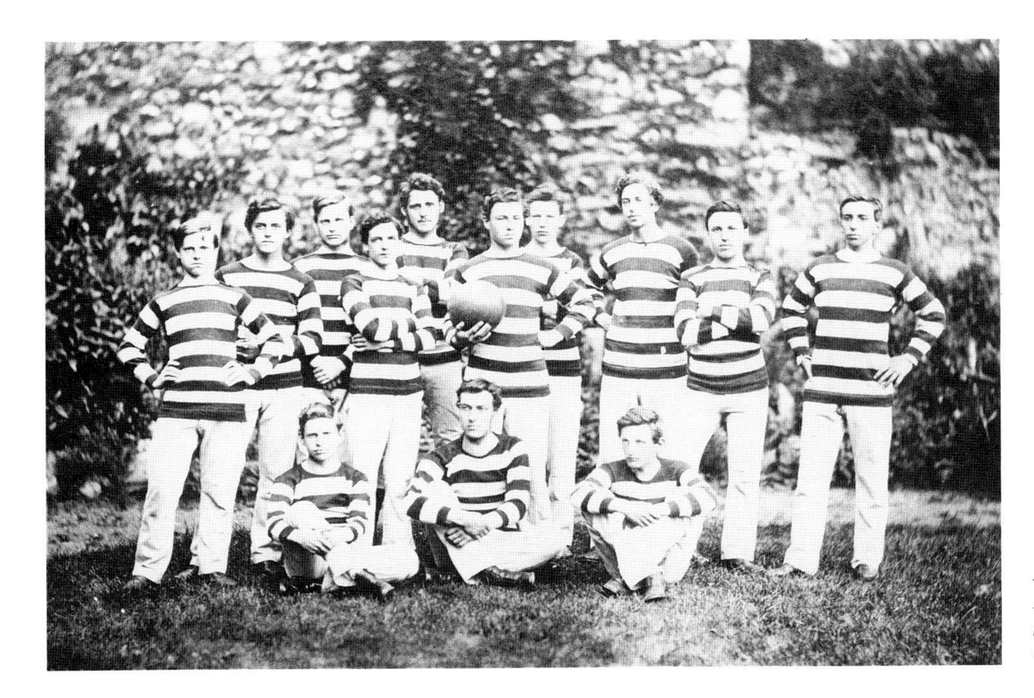

The Football XIII of 1872/3. Although the School joined the Rugby Union in 1872 the new code took some time to displace the Canterbury game altogether.

> considered the conduct of the Sixth "overbearing". . . . There were therefore expelled from the Football Club and their subscriptions returned [eleven names follow]. In consequence of this diminution of force, when a match was played on the 5th November with the Clergy Orphan School . . . the COS got 5 games while the King's School did not obtain one. It must be remembered also that during the playing of the match, some of those that had been expelled . . . rendered themselves unenviably conspicuous by clapping and showing pleasure when the King's School lost a game.'

The incident is another example of resentment by the boys of the school at the introduction of foreign customs. Mitchinson was apparently trying to give the sixth form the sort of status it had at Rugby.

Mosse's nostalgic account of the school and its characters is not entirely reconcilable with the account which its best known boy of the period, Somerset Maugham, gives in his autobiographical novel, *Of Human Bondage*. Maugham arrived at the Junior School towards the end of Blore's time and writes that Blore (whom he names Dr Fleming) had become so deaf that his wife had to shout words he missed into his ear. The full story of Blore's decline is more bizarre; he finally became so confused that on one occasion his trusted parlour-maid had to persuade him that the High Street was not the proper place to prepare for bed.

Blore had had previous troubles. For several months in 1879 he was on sick-leave, probably as a result of strain caused by negotiating a new regulating scheme for the school which had come into force the previous year. The new scheme formally separated the functions of the Dean and Chapter as the school's Governing Body from their other functions. It also defined the respective responsibilities of the Dean and Chapter and the headmaster. It is on this subject that the negotiations – which had begun as early as Mitchinson's time – could have proved stressful for Blore.

Somerset Maugham, wearing his probationer King's Scholar's gown. In 1889 he was in the Fifth Form, aged 15.

Maugham's suggestion that the masters of the school hoped Hodgson would be chosen as Blore's successor, and were much alarmed when the Dean and Chapter chose Tom Perkins (the name he gives to the Revd Thomas Field) is credible.

'At first nobody knew who Perkins was, and the name favourably impressed no one; but before the shock of it had passed away, it was realised that Perkins was the son of Perkins the linen-draper. . . .' The masters present on this occasion, Maugham continues, 'have been known to generations of schoolboys as Sighs, Tar, Winks, Squirts, and Pat.

'They all knew Tom Perkins. The first thing about him was that he was not a gentleman. . . . He was a small, dark boy, with untidy black hair and large eyes. He looked like a gypsy. He had come to the school as a day-boy, with the best scholarship on the endowment, so that his education had cost him nothing. Of course he was brilliant. At every Speech-Day he was loaded with prizes. He was their show-boy. . . .'

'But there was quite a difference between welcoming his [more recent] success at other schools and serving under his leadership in their own. Tar had frequently given him lines, and Squirts had boxed his ears. They could not imagine how the Chapter had made such a mistake.'

Not only was it true that Field was the son of a bankrupt linen-draper, but Maugham barely changes the nicknames of the masters of the time. Sighs was R. B. Gordon, Tar was L. G. H. Mason, Winks was Canon L. H. Evans and Pat was W. Price. Only Squirts (E. J. Campbell) was in fact known as 'Scrags'.

Perkins's least popular innovation was his habit of announcing suddenly that

Thomas Field with the Sixth Form of 1889.

he would take one of the other masters' forms for a lesson. Then all would be turned upside down; boys top of the class for their construing of the classics would be displaced in Perkins's list of marks by one who knew who General Gordon was.

Maugham's young hero, Philip, goes first into the class of Squirts. Of Squirts Maugham writes with bitterness: 'No master could have been more unfitted to teach things to so shy a boy as Philip.' Philip is reduced by Squirts to terrified silence, and sent to the headmaster for the Black Book. The Black Book can be seen today, with Maugham's name in it. The only change he makes to history is to alter his real offence, 'Gross Inattention' to Philip's more heroic 'Gross insubordination'.

It is when Perkins casually mentions that he, as a boy, has had the same treatment from Squirts that he begins to receive Philip's 'dog-like adoration'. And though in the end Philip disappoints Perkins by refusing to go to university and be ordained, the picture Maugham gives of Perkins remains a highly sympathetic one.

About the other masters he is disrespectful rather than vindictive. Tar, he writes, 'was a short man with an immense belly, a black beard turning now to grey, and a swarthy skin. In his clerical dress there was indeed something in him to suggest the tar-barrel; and though on principle he gave five hundred lines to any boy on whose lips he overheard his nickname, at dinner parties in the precincts he often made little jokes about it. He was the most worldly of the masters . . . . He liked a bottle of wine and a good dinner, and having once been seen at the Café Royal with a lady who was very probably a near relation, was thenceforward supposed by generations of schoolboys to indulge in orgies the circumstantial details of which pointed to an unbounded belief in human depravity.'

Some of Maugham's general comments on the school are exaggerated, as an examination of the register has shown, if not by much. 'During the three centuries since its separation from the monastic order,' he writes, 'it had trained especially men of the church, bishops, deans, canons, and above all country clergymen: there were boys in the school whose fathers, grandfathers, great-grandfathers, had been educated there and had all been rectors of parishes in the diocese of Tercanbury; and they came to it with their minds made up already to be ordained. But there were signs notwithstanding that even there changes were coming; for a few,

The Revd L. G. H. Mason – '*Tar*' *for tar-barrel – and (right) the Revd R. G. Hodgson, Lower Master, in about 1890.*

	Wed.	Wigram	Continued bad work all [illegible]	[illegible]
8th	Friday	Temple (3 times)	Continual Idleness & neglect of work	[illegible]
8th	Friday	Maugham	Gross Inattention	[illegible]
9th	Saturday	Kingdon	Bad Gk. Exercise	[illegible]
		Robinson	Not giving up an Exercise and not telling me	[illegible]
11th	Monday	Temple.	Disgraceful work in [illegible]	[illegible]
14th	Thursday	Ashenden	Repeated misbehaviour.	[illegible]
15th	Friday	Carter	Impertinence	[illegible]
		Page	Talking in class	[illegible]

The Black Book. Three entries sentenced the offender to a Headmaster's beating but the humane Field seldom felt bound by this. Four lines below Maugham appears Ashenden, the name used by the narrator of many of Maugham's stories.

repeating what they had heard at home, said that the Church was no longer what it used to be. It wasn't so much the money; but the class of people who went in for it weren't the same; and two or three boys knew curates whose fathers were tradesmen; they'd rather go out to the Colonies . . . .'

But about Field's enlivening influence Maugham was undoubtedly right. He especially encouraged swimming and boating on the Stour. 'One can see him now,' L. H. Evans (Winks) writes, 'jumping overboard and struggling up to the neck in the water to wrench out one of the stakes that the local angling association had driven into the river bed in the hope of stopping the passage of boats.'

It is surprising that, along with so much that was liberal, Field should have introduced the first item of school uniform, the straw hat. For this Harrow – he had been assistant master there before returning to Canterbury – was his model, indeed he even wrote for the school a Harrow-style old school song which the boys ignored. A more civilizing innovation was his dividing of the school into 'tutor sets', each set made up of boys of all ages. The purpose of these, Field noted, was to put each boy into contact throughout his school time with another master besides the headmaster. The duty of this master, to be known as the tutor, was to 'make a special study of a boy's character morally and intellectually and to preserve the continuous thread of the boy's history in the school'. The tutor was to stimulate the boy's outside reading and to help him 'so far as may be permissible' with his entries for prizes or scholarships. He was also to act as something of a protector. No serious punishment was to be set, nor was a boy to be sent to the headmaster without the tutor's knowledge. Tutor sets are still a feature of the school today.

As Maugham suggests, when Field taught he invariably encouraged what would be today called lateral thinking. 'If he were taking us to Geography,' one boy writes, 'the place literally lived before us. Its historical associations were interwoven – so that we used to say that his favourite question ran: "Now in connection with that, who watted whom, where?" '

Racing in Fours at Fordwich at the turn of the century. Straw hats were the first items of School uniform at King's.

Above all it was Field's informality which was remembered when he died, an old man, in 1936. 'I can hear him now,' L. H. Evans writes, 'in the Mint Yard (when starting out to play golf) shouting in stentorian tones to his manservant in an upper room: "Taylor! lend me half-a-crown." I can see him (before his marriage!) after inviting some of the masters to listen to a talk on music by John Farmer and finding a shortage of chairs, rushing into the room with a hip-bath and a rug to make up the deficiency.'

The Revd Arthur Galpin, who succeeded Field when he went to Radley as warden in 1896, was neither comfortably lovable like Blore nor excitingly lovable like Field, but he was in many ways an excellent headmaster. By the time he retired in 1910 the school's numbers had increased by over 100 and become stabilized at around 250. He accommodated this larger number by opening several town houses.

He also added a new wing to the Grange with laboratories, dormitories, and masters' rooms. And he added the Harvey Laboratory to the Alford Laboratory in the Mint Yard. He encouraged the writing of the first history of the school by Woodruff and Cape, an old King's Scholar and a member of the staff, respectively. The result could hardly have been bettered, even by the historian of English education, Arthur Leach, who offered to write it, but lost interest when told there were no good golf clubs near Canterbury. A previous attempt to write the school's history had been undertaken, with the encouragement of Mitchinson, by the Revd J. S. Sidebotham, but he had been frustrated by the cathedral auditor, Mr Finch, who refused to make records available, telling Sidebotham that he 'did not know what use might be made of the information'. As a result it consists mainly of biographies of King's Scholars, and though these are of much interest, does not tell a coherent story.

The New Wing was added to The Grange in 1900. Eventually Galpin had to pay half the cost out of his own pocket.

Horace Spence, though not yet senior enough to wear a wing collar, has exceptionally well-stocked book and jam shelves as well as privacy. Mitchinson revolutionised, his successors civilised.

Above all Galpin raised the school's academic standards to their highest level in modern times, partly by recruiting good staff, partly by his own teaching, partly by further broadening its curriculum. In a single week in 1907 boys of the school won four university scholarships or exhibitions, in classics, mathematics, modern history, and natural science.

Galpin himself remains a difficult man to picture. He came to the school with a wider background and more varied interests than some clerical academics. True he had won the expected first class degrees in classics at Oxford and had most recently been a housemaster at Marlborough, but he had also played in his school, Sherborne's, Rugby XV for three years, and been for two years a member of the Oxford shooting VIII. Among his other interests were music (he played the cello) and archaeology. Immediately after leaving Oxford he had gone for a year and a half to Canada as tutor to the sons of the Governor General. It is odd that such a man should have left so few vivid personal impressions at Canterbury.

In 1956 an old boy, S. S. Sopwith, wrote about his classroom style: 'Galpin would come in on the stroke of the clock with a dignified but brisk purposefulness, and glance rapidly round the silent and apprehensive form . . . as if he were welcoming us all to a party'. But Sopwith admits that Galpin was not generally liked. He was known as 'Oily', a word which the letter he wrote to the Archbishop of Canterbury when sending him a copy of Woodruff and Cape's history indeed suggests. Another old boy, A. B. Emden, considered that he 'lacked the personal touch that is so important in a Housemaster – and he was Housemaster of half the school'.

Galpin was still only 50 when, in 1910, for no obvious reason, he retired. Perhaps he felt unappreciated. Like Blore and Field, he had spent considerable amounts of his own money on the school, giving £1000 and lending another £500 to its building fund. He took the living of Saltwood, a small village now a suburb of Hythe, but with a good stipend and desirable parsonage – perhaps these tempted him. Saltwood has another connection with Canterbury. It was in its great ruined castle that the four knights plotted the night before they set off to murder Becket.

Galpin (third master from the right) on the eve of his 1910 retirement. The School look in very good shape, orderly but – observe the little devil – not dragooned.

10

WORLD WAR AND DEPRESSION

BETWEEN 1910 AND 1927 THE SCHOOL'S REPUTATION AND ACADEMIC STANDARDS DECLINED FROM THE HIGH POINT THEY HAD REACHED UNDER GALPIN. AN OLD BOY, J. N. B. LAINÉ, there in the last five of these years, considered that it had become probably the last surviving school to resemble the Rugby of *Tom Brown's Schooldays*. For this fossilization the two headmasters were responsible. During the following eight years it slid into financial crisis. For this the Depression and the inability of the governors to cope with it must be blamed.

It is easy to sympathize with the Revd C. R. L. McDowall (1910–16) and

Dean Wace, parasol-shaded, addresses the Officer Training Corps in the Mint Yard. King's Birthday Parade, 27th May 1911.

Algernon Latter (1916–27). Both were devoted to the school and well liked. But one was overwhelmed by events of his time, the other failed to see problems ahead. McDowall was the more unfortunate. He was an old-fashioned, quiet man, who might have been able, in ordinary circumstances, to sustain the well-regarded and successful school he had inherited. But the circumstances soon ceased to be ordinary, and he was unable to bear the slaughter of his ex-pupils, both those from Canterbury and from his previous house at Eton. By the time he left he was, according to Edwards, close to a nervous breakdown.

A boy of McDowall's time, C. E. A. Pullan, who was indeed killed on the Western Front at the end of 1915, left an incomplete account of the school which was later published by his father. Whatever its incipient defects, Pullan was happy there. 'This last year of one's school life', he wrote, 'is something to look back upon when life is a little toilsome, with a singularly perfect recollection.'

The worship of athletics heroes, signficantly called 'bloods', was by now the school's emotional centre. Rugby was more popular than cricket, but the members of any school team which won a match were applauded as they came into the Big Schoolroom the following morning. 'Bloods' alone were allowed to sit on the seat around the tree in the Mint Yard. Pullan lists the other regulations, mainly of dress, which the senior boys imposed on the junior (as at other schools of the time), particularly the width and colour of the ribbons of their straw hats. It was the privilege of a sixth former to carry a walking stick.

Olympus – the 'Bloods' Bench' under the Mint Yard lime tree.

A contemporary of Pullan's, D. S. Stainer, who survived the war and later became a member of the staff, gives another view of the school's athletic heroes. In the School House, where he was a boarder, there was one study which 'housed a rather curious community, people who through athletic prowess had attained 'Bloodhood' but whose academic status was disproportionately low; one or two of them were actually in Form 3c. They were a happy-go-lucky crowd, who enjoyed life unhampered by worries about university scholarships. . . . It was they who always conducted the annual sweepstakes on the Derby and the Cesarewitch'.

Stainer describes the ceremonial commencement of Morning Prayers in the Big Schoolroom. 'First, ordinary people assembled, then, in ones and twos, the Sixth Form passed through us and disappeared into the Rabbit Hutch. In the meantime the masters had all assembled in the Headmaster's House. With the Headmaster in the van accompanied by his senior assistant, a man of very striking presence, extremely stout with a large square beard, the masters would emerge, and proceed through the Mint Yard, and up the steps to the Big Schoolroom, whereupon the Sixth Form would emerge from the Rabbit Hutch and the ceremony of "nibs" [prayers] commence.

'The procession of masters . . . made a fine picture, the black-gowned figures, some tall, some short, some fat, some lean, some spruce, some shabby, some erect, some bowed – it reminded one of the Pied Piper of Hamlyn. A man I knew desired very much to draw this procession, and in the interests of art was deliberately late on several occasions, he usually got a friend to answer his name, but sometimes he was unfortunate. . . .'

By 1914 Stainer was in the form of Nathaniel Goss, later the lower master. One morning Goss read to the class *The Times*'s leading article on the murder of the Archduke Ferdinand at Sarajevo. 'The article was well written, and Mr Goss enjoyed reading out the beautifully rounded periods. We enjoyed it, too: it was a pleasant change from being called upon to construe ill-prepared passages of Horace. . . . We were pleasantly excited. There might even be a war . . . .'

In the war which followed 850 old boys served, 135 died, 1 won the V.C, 57 the DSO and 106 the MC – high numbers from a school of only about 250 boys.

Algernon Latter (brother-in-law of the 'bearded and muscular' Hodgson) was 'a tall rather gaunt, impressive man, with sunken eyes which seemed to pierce one from below heavy eyebrows', W. d'A. Maycock writes: 'So far as I recall I never heard any boy utter hard words about "Algy".' The Revd G. I. Soden considers that he owed a permanent debt of gratitude to "Algy" and remembers that he 'felt only shame and not resentment when he remarked to me one day, "You look very spotty" '. But the school over which he presided was Spartan. In School House, J. N. B. Lainé remembers being 'abominably fed' with nothing after tea except for a cup of soup at 9 p.m. There was also 'not a little bullying'.

The trouble lay in Latter's extreme conservatism, symbolized by his enormous moustache. On Corps days he would exhort the boys to be worthy of an empire on which the sun never set. The school must remain the school it had been in the great imperial days when he himself attended it. Why should the boys need a gramophone when boys of his time hadn't? – useless to tell him that it hadn't then been invented. Sunday Matins still began at 10.30 a.m. and did not end until

PLATE 11
Top: William Butterfield's clock tower at St Augustine's seen through a window in the Tudor garden wall.

Bottom: Blackfriars, the refectory of the Dominican house established on both banks of the Stour in the 13th century, houses the art room, various craft activities and the Cleary Gallery.

PLATE 12 Walking through the Godmersham Arch, brought to the School in 1957 to open a way to the Shirley Hall.

Lords of Hosts: Captain Latter briefs Archbishop Randall Davidson with Dr Galpin and Captain Bell in reserve. OTC Parade on Blore's, 1909.

about 12.50 p.m. There was no end to the worship of games and their heroes. And if corporal punishment did not take as long, it was ritualized. Derek Ingram Hill (author of *The Six Preachers of Canterbury Cathedral*), who was in The Grange, remembers how, at the appropriate moment before breakfast, the two canes known as Rosemary and Isobella would be brought from the mid-front study of School House and ceremonially carried across the Mint Yard.

It was in Latter's time that Alaric Jacob arrived at the school – a member of the family whose sixteenth-century ancestor had founded Jacobopolis (see page 22). In 1930, aged seventeen, Jacob published a novel with the title *Seventeen*, as closely based on the King's School as Somerset Maugham's *Of Human Bondage* had been. Alec Waugh's *Loom of Youth* had appeared 13 years earlier and the message of *Seventeen* is similar: that it is hypocritical to pretend emotional friendships do not develop at an all-boys' boarding school. At Furlington – the name Jacob gives the King's School – they are referred to as 'cases'. Today this seems neither surprising nor particularly shocking. At least as shocking are his descriptions of the masters of the school, a dismaying collection of decrepits and incompetents. He probably exaggerates, but his criticism is never shrill and the novel is remarkably mature for a boy of that age.

Towards the end of Latter's time the Governing Body, largely at the suggestion of Dean Bell, approved a highly significant expansion of itself (typically, Latter dissented from the otherwise unanimous vote). In future there were to be four 'outside' governors, two co-opted by the Dean and Chapter, one appointed by Trinity College, Oxford, one by Corpus Christi College, Cambridge. Three of

Captain of the XV. After a good 1923/4 season C. H. Gibson went on to an Oxford Blue and a County cap.

these new governors were to play key parts in the dramatic happenings which soon enveloped – and but for them would have engulfed – the school.

The event which precipitated matters might have been as fortunate as any in the school's history – the gift to it of Sturry Court. This old manor lay two and a half miles to the north-east of the cathedral, in the Stour valley; it already had a connection with the school. John Twyne, the headmaster whose reign spanned the Reformation, had set the symposium which forms his remarkable book, *De Rebus Albionicis*, at Sturry Court. At that time, the 1530s, it had belonged to St Augustine's Abbey. A few years later when the abbey was dissolved the last abbot, who is the book's central speaker, was allowed to continue living there (*in luctu et squalore*, according to Twyne – despite his generous pension of £133 a year).

Sturry Court was eventually bought in 1906 by Alfred Milner, High Commissioner in South Africa. It was when Milner died childless in 1925 that his widow presented the manor and surrounding six acres of land to the King's School, believing that a school would be an appropriate memorial to her husband and his well-known 'kindergarten' of young colonial administrators. Somewhat dizzied by this generous gift, the Governing Body considered moving most of the school to Sturry Court, but eventually decided that it should become the Junior School.

Plans were drawn up for a great new building in the manor's grounds. 'I well remember', A. B. Emden, one of the new 'outside' governors writes, 'my amazement on seeing the already accepted architect's plans that were on view at the first meeting of the Governing Body that I attended.' They were modified: two wings of the new H-shaped block were never built and a vast swimming pool was reduced to half its size. But the cost of what *was* built left the school hopelessly in debt.

No money remained for what was by this time urgent: the refurbishing of the main school's accommodation to bring it up to the standard of its competitors.

Rudyard Kipling was the speaker at the opening of Milner Court on 5 October 1929. Here he is with N. P. Birley behind Archbishop Lang. He thought the boys' accommodation in the rather gaunt buildings inclined to luxury.

And the school could not borrow more since it did not own its main buildings and so had nothing to offer as security.

Nor did it own, with the exception of Blore's Piece, any playing fields. This at least Norman Birley, who succeeded Latter in 1927, put right by buying with a mortgage St Stephen's Fields, now known as Birley's. His regime was a civilizing one. He put a stop to the systematic 'harrying and actual bullying' of new boys including so-called 'newboy concerts' and to the fagging of new boys by those only just their seniors. He also separated the Grange from School House, and allowed scholars to board there, or in the two outhouses in the city. The Captain of the School might now come from any of its houses. But these improvements did not touch the school's financial problems. When they were faced it was realized that £25 000 would be needed to modernize the buildings, and that the school could never be run economically unless the number of boarders was increased from 168 to 250. Old boys, when appealed to, raised £10 000 and the Ecclesiastical Commissioners contributed £5000, but by now the school had debts of £40 000–60 000 and was making an annual loss of £6000. For end-of-term payments its full overdraft facility had to be used and the bank would lend no more.

Meanwhile, Dean Bell, whose enthusiasm for Sturry Court was responsible for the school's problems (though it was a time when more professional financiers made similar mistakes), had become Bishop of Chichester, leaving the canons leaderless and infected with a pessimism about the school's future which, in Emden's words, they 'freely expressed'. By the time Birley left in 1935 to become headmaster of the Merchant Taylors' School, bankruptcy was close.

11

CANON SHIRLEY AND AFTER

WHATEVER HAPPENS IN THE NEXT TEN YEARS, F. J. SHIRLEY, THE MAN WHO SUCCEEDED BIRLEY IN 1935, MUST REMAIN THE KING'S SCHOOL'S HEADMASTER OF THE century. Without Shirley, the school would have foundered or become unrecognizably changed. Today, almost 30 years since Shirley retired, the present headmaster will say in unguarded moments that he still considers it his most important duty to free the school from his overshadowing influence.

The school's dismaying situation early in 1935 is well shown by a letter which Dr Hewlett Johnson, the Red Dean, wrote to parents, at a time when Shirley had been appointed but not yet arrived. Johnson not only writes with warm approval of public schools and the education they provide (things he elsewhere deplores) but begs parents to continue to send their boys to the school. Many had been removing them at sixteen, and he quotes extensively from a statement by the Royal Commission of the Civil Service advising against this practice. He even begs a few parents to leave their boys at the school although they are old enough to leave, 'to give the school that leadership which its present position so urgently craves'.

F.J.S.

Shirley was the candidate (no other was considered) of two of the outside governors, A. B. Emden (O.K.S.) of St Edmund Hall, Oxford, and Will Spens, Master of Corpus Christi College, Cambridge. Emden knew him well – St Edmund Hall had been Shirley's college. He had visited him at Worksop College, where Shirley had been headmaster for ten years, watching him unseen as he worked with the school's dramatic society. Worksop was the only independent school which was actually prospering in these Depression years. Emden and Spens had no doubt that Shirley was the one man who could save the King's School.

It was another of the outside governors, Lord Justice Luxmoore (O.K.S.), a man with powerful political friends, who engineered a condition on which Shirley insisted, and which helped to make recovery possible: that he should become a canon of the cathedral. This freed the school from matching Shirley's Worksop salary, and from providing him with a house, so releasing the headmaster's large house in the Mint Yard for conversion into a boys' house. Still more important, it gave Shirley a seat on the Chapter (as distinct from the school's Governing Body) where most of the important decisions about the school's premises were taken. But it was Shirley himself who found more fundamental solutions for the school's problems.

How did he do it? His first and most controversial move – sometimes called the rape of Worksop – was to persuade the parents of about 30 of his Worksop boys to send them with him to Canterbury. Furthermore, they would continue to pay Worksop fees of £150 a year, not King's School fees of £135. Behaviour of this sort had precedents. In the eighteenth century (see page 43) a candidate for the headmastership had offered to do something similar which might have been called the rape of Ashford if the dean had appointed him. But many people were shocked, and Shirley was suspended from the Headmasters' Conference. Many years later Shirley defended himself in the most forthright way.

> 'I did *not* wrongly take boys from Worksop. In ten and a half years I had made that cheap and bankrupt school into a wealthy state: the numbers rose from 200 to over 400 . . .: the fees from £90 to £150; I had built much more than half the school that now stands, which, with modernising the rest, cost fully £100,000. My reign . . . included the slumps of 1928 and 1931 . . . and Worksop was the only school in the land to increase its numbers and raise its fees and build extensive buildings during those years. . . . My grip was personal – I drew boys from all over England, whereas up to 1925 they'd all been Midlands and North – the parents thought the world of *me*, and when they knew in 1935 that I was going to Canterbury, many wanted their sons to accompany me. I discussed this with the Worksop Governors – who begged me to stay, offered me another 15 years' agreement with far more salary and a very large pension – and we had a formal agreement in writing that I was to have thirty and no more, that a large percentage of the thirty would be boys that had entered but not yet come, and that I would fill the places of all I took and leave W'sop with the numbers it would have had, had I been staying. *This I did*, and among my papers I have that agreement which will also be in the W'sop archives.'

Shirley's action still suggests the house tenant who rolls up the turfs of his lawn to take them with him when he moves; his defence shows that, once committed to his new job, his loyalty to it was so complete that he could ignore the principle that however long and successfully you work for an employer you acquire no right to a slice of his business.

Shirley was soon proved correct in diagnosing the school's most essential need to have been more pupils. In the following year it made a profit. This enabled him to suggest to the Dean and Chapter his financial master stroke. He told them that the school no longer needed the £1000 a year which they contributed to its scholarships and staff salaries and would accept in return a once-and-for-all lump sum. They took professional advice and agreed to pay the school nearly £26 000.

Shirley had already accommodated the boys from Worksop, together with the boys of Langley House, one of the town outhouses, in Walpole House, which he established in the old Junior School building near the Archbishop's Palace. He chose the name, not because Hugh Walpole (an old boy of the school) contributed – though he did later pay for the turfing of the Mint Yard – but to associate the school with such a well-known writer. Now he had money to start the great building and modernizing programme which transformed the school's premises over the next five years. Early in this was the renting from the Dean and Chapter of Meister Omers, which took boys from Holme House, the other outhouse, and meant that the school's boarders could now be entirely accommodated within the Precincts.

But to explain Shirley's success in terms of money and buildings is to miss its essence, which lay in his single-minded commitment to every aspect of the school's revival. He made the boys well aware of this, and drew them, like everyone else, into working for it. One old boy, John Goudge, remembers Shirley's

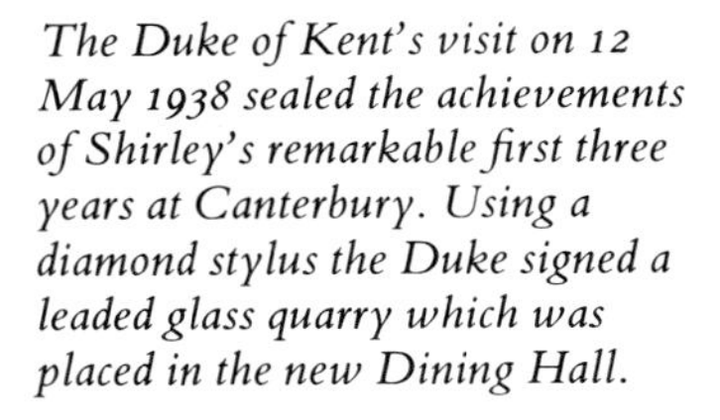

The Duke of Kent's visit on 12 May 1938 sealed the achievements of Shirley's remarkable first three years at Canterbury. Using a diamond stylus the Duke signed a leaded glass quarry which was placed in the new Dining Hall.

> 'harangues to the assembled school in what was then the Big Schoolroom. . . . Often in 1935/36 his subject was the dangerous state the school was in. He made no bones about it, saying that it had been almost broke, he was doing what he could to pull it together – and we must do our part – by acting as ambassadors, by backing him up and, above all, by passing examinations and winning scholarships and matches. There was little that any individual could do except try a little harder. But his passionate appeals did much to weld us together and inspire a corporate spirit'.

Though on these occasions Shirley spoke to the school, as it were, from above, he was the opposite of a distant figure. 'We were astonished', Goudge continues,

> 'at how he treated us as equals. Many of us weren't equipped to deal with this. He seemed to be thinking aloud and at the same time seeking sympathy. Usually no response was demanded and we simply listened in wonder, flattered by his confidences. His normal form of address was "m'dear". He was genuinely fond of the company of boys. It occurs to me that he may have been a lonely man; that his associates may have been too wary of his power of personality ever to become intimate and so he may have lacked the real friends that most of us need to trust and confide in. Perhaps he met this need to some extent by talking to his boys. If there was any homosexual element in this relationship it was completely under control and we were not embarrassed by it.'

Shirley had married in 1926 – his daughter became the first, and at the time the only, girl in the school.

Goudge describes Shirley (always 'Fred' to the boys) as

> 'of medium height and build, with a very slight indication of a paunch. His feet and hands were small, almost delicately so. . . . He had a curious habit of blinking as he looked at you . . . it almost seemed as if he was punctuating his sentences with his eyes . . . his words were often preceded by a pursing of the lips and an exhalation through the nose, accompanied by a kind of humming sound which could be taken as a sign of approval, astonishment, ridicule, disbelief, amusement or anger, depending on the circumstances. He smoked cigarettes, but he didn't deliberately inhale; in fact, he rarely took the cigarette out of his mouth, preferring to let it burn, inhaling naturally as he breathed and letting the ash drop on his waistcoat'.

Shirley's openness reached a climax in the monitors' meetings he would hold during the war. James Breese, a contemporary of Goudge's, remembers 'how he used these meetings to talk about himself, his anxiety about his health, his feelings that he had achieved little in life, and no doubt other worries and concerns. Isolated as many of those at the top are, he yet had the openness to use these meetings for a mixture of the confessional and the kind of disclosure of inner feelings more commonly displayed in group therapy'.

It would be easy to collect enough of such memories to make Shirley sound not merely a remarkable character but a warped one. For example, Tom Stapleton writes, 'it was strange that one so intelligent should make regular trips to London for colonic washouts'. The way in which he involved himself in school plays was equally curious. At Worksop (the boys of Canterbury were told) he would choose a play and 'let the staff and boys get on with it until about a fortnight before the actual performance, when he would . . . announce that so and so was "hopeless", and, as it was far too late to rehearse a replacement, he would have to take the part himself. It would be one he had had his eye on all the time, and not a minor part either'.

On one occasion, sitting with a guest in the audience of a school *Hamlet*, Shirley was informed that the Gravedigger was indisposed, and slipped out to play the part himself. When he returned his guest told him, 'Oh what a pity, you've just missed the most marvellous Gravedigger I've ever seen'. Shirley's interventions were not always so successful. Once he 'so flustered the cast of *Sir Thomas More* [his own edition of the supposed Shakespeare play] that they went through most of one scene twice. . . . The reason was the over-generous helpings of claret he had administered beforehand to get them in the mood'.

Under Shirley corporal punishment of various degrees was still very much part of the school's routine. John Moss, another contemporary, remembers Shirley's Lower Vb Latin class – classics was his subject. 'One day Shirley appeared without his cane and we all sighed with relief. The relief was shortlived because, as soon as someone transgressed, he dived down into the wings of his gown, and like a conjurer, produced it with a triumphant smile . . . .' He had 'the disconcerting habit of standing behind whoever was translating and giving him a sharp thwack across the shoulders at each mistake; not too fierce, just enough to raise a little dust'.

Goudge tells how he and another boy, Neville Hearne, were beaten by Shirley during their last few weeks at the school. They were

> 'summoned to see him . . . after we had gone to bed. He taxed us with slackness and setting a bad example and challenged us to deny we had been smoking. Neither of us bothered to deny it. Having given us a lecture he announced that he was going to beat us – highly unusual for such senior boys – we could, if we wished, refuse to submit, but in that case he would expel us. This threat in the circumstances was quite unreasonable. We didn't believe he would carry it out, but we hadn't the nerve to call his bluff and . . . agreed to take the beating. The room was full of furniture: cupboards, a table, chairs, bookshelves and a bed. There simply wasn't room to swing a cane properly, so each of us in turn had to bend over the bed and was beaten gently – 37 strokes. It didn't hurt at first, but the cumulative effect was considerable and the pain towards the end excruciating. We hadn't been expecting anything like it and the shock was severe, not least because of the calculating and cunning way it was done. . . . Subsequent thought about the occasion – and it was not one to be easily forgotten – confirmed in my mind that it was indeed a sadistic act.'

Extravaganza.

Shirley could also seem a snob. Tony Eyre believes that one of the things which saved him from a beating after being caught by Shirley at a cinema was his name. 'That week *Picture Post* had an article on the Society of Genealogists, with a full page photo of a man holding a scroll, captioned "Seven feet of the family of Eyre, a family worth belonging to". When I confirmed that we had a tree going back to the Normans, he was all over me. From that day on, I was a programme seller at every school play etc., together with Bonham-Carter and one or two others whose names he liked to see in print on the programme itself.' But a story of this sort does not catch the complexity of his character. Certainly the romantic idea of a family with a long history appealed to him, but when he used boys with aristocratic names to publicize the school it was less because he was a snob himself than to appeal to the snobbery of others, at whom – as well as at himself – he was really laughing.

Shirley's calculating determination that the school should win football and cricket matches as well as scholarships was transparent. He would 'shout instructions and also express his disgust and despair' from touchline and pavilion, 'but he had no real knowledge of any of the games we played. His sole concern was the prestige of the school and we were made to feel his bitter disappointment when we failed. . . . There were fierce accusations of slackness. . . . He couldn't understand, why, in cricket, if you could make 10, you couldn't make 20 . . .'.

Determined to get results, he recruited the famous retired Kent and England professional, Frank Woolley to coach the school at cricket. Woolley was 'a man of very few words indeed,' Goudge writes,

> 'practically monosyllabic; and this, combined with the unique quality of his art, which was at once inimitable and incommunicable, undoubtedly limited his value as a coach. He used to stand around silently while we got on with our practice, occasionally taking a bat and going through the motions of a stroke; and this simply didn't measure up to most people's idea of what he should have been doing, especially Canon Shirley's. There was something about Frank's languid manner that infuriated the Headmaster, who couldn't understand why he didn't "get on with the job".'

The remarkable fact remains that Shirley's behaviour of this sort, some of it discreditable, some of which suggests that he was a monster, had little effect on his popularity with the boys of the school which, after a few years, became almost universal. Two explanations are mentioned again and again by those who remember him. The first is his genuine concern for them, not as a group but individually. Breese remembers taking to Shirley his entry application for a Cambridge college. 'Within half an hour or so I was entered for an Oxford college . . . I forget his reasoning . . . it is his concern that I recall – I felt important to him.' Michael Mayne, today's Dean of Westminster, has told how Shirley changed his life. 'He didn't persuade me with clever words. He simply wrote me a letter in which he said, "You're not going to be an actor, you're going to be a priest".' The second is the excitement he invariably produced. Even in saying routine prayers he would make 'electric pauses'. As Goudge sums it up, 'when he appeared on the scene everyone stopped doing what they were doing, agog for what might happen'.

All around them the boys saw evidence of Shirley's ability to stimulate governors and bankers.

> 'Every term we came back to find new developments and daring innovations. In 1937 alone, less than two years after Shirley took over, the Field Classrooms were opened, along with the swimming pool and squash courts on Blore's; hard tennis courts, now superseded by the Shirley Hall, appeared behind the Grange; Lattergate opened and Langley House became the sanatorium; Marlowe moved into the monastic bakehouse and brewhouse. In 1938, along with the Big Schoolroom's masterly transformation into the Library, came the Dining Hall, one of Shirley's most brilliant improvisations.'

The war brought Shirley's great expansion programme to a temporary halt when the school was evacuated to Cornwall. He describes what happened.

> 'I secured a very large hotel, the Carlyon Bay Hotel in Cornwall, near St Austell, together with a smaller hotel . . . two large Georgian houses three miles apart, and about ten other houses of varying size. . . . The school, though mostly concentrated on the two hotels, was nevertheless widely scattered.
>
> 'I took with me the King's School, our own Junior School, the Cathedral Choir School, and the Senior and Junior Schools of St Edmund's School, Canterbury, who could not afford to move on their own. . . . The whole formed one School under my charge and responsibility for the five and a quarter years we were there.

Fun with pitchforks and gasmasks in the early weeks of the War.

The King's Scholars process in front of the Carlyon Bay Hotel, the School's wartime home, in the summer of 1940.

Another Canterbury custom transplanted to Cornwall: Punishment Drill with Sgt. Major Marshall ('Barch') under monitorial aegis.

'The evacuation took place in May 1940, accomplished fully in eight days. I sent all boys home from Canterbury with instructions to catch the night train from Paddington on the eighth day; they would arrive at Par and buses would bring them the two miles to Carlyon Bay in time for breakfast. Thirty senior boys stayed with me, and loaded up railway vans and road lorries with all the furniture and books and equipment; they went down to Cornwall on the last load, and had everything unpacked and placed *in situ* for the arrival of boys and masters and matrons at breakfast-time on the appointed morning. They were wonderful boys – and within two years some of them were killed in action.

'There were no classrooms, no laboratories, no playing-fields. The first summer all teaching was done out of doors; but by winter I had converted a dozen breeze-block single garages into classrooms, erected a breeze-block single physics laboratory, bought and transported from Truro an enormous wooden shed which made three chemistry laboratories, and leased the Cornish Riviera Club – sited on the beach – for some classroom accommodation, and for the indoor tennis courts it possessed. . . .

'The centre of our communal life was the large garage of the hotel – it could and did hold 600 to 700 people. That was our chapel – we brought the altar from home, which was screened off when the garage became a theatre, or a lecture hall, or a concert room. . . . The floor, of course, sloped to the drains necessary for washing down cars, and the roof was of corrugated iron. But there we had school prayers every day, and services on every Sunday; and there very many distinguished people came to speak to or to entertain these 600 boys . . .'.

In 1945 Shirley brought back to Canterbury more King's School boys than he had taken away. There was less room for them. Many bombs had fallen on the city, particularly in the Baedeker raids of 1–4 June 1942. The most serious losses to the school were the headmaster's house in the Precincts, the dining hall and the new block of classrooms Shirley had built. Bombs had also made two boarding houses uninhabitable. 'Two other boarding houses had been inhabited by the soldiery' reducing them to 'almost as bad a condition as if they had been bombed.' As for the Assembly Hall in the Mint Yard (known as the Parry, after Bishop Parry), this had become a British Restaurant, which the city was reluctant to surrender. Nevertheless, by the summer of 1946 the school was able to receive the King and Queen at its formal re-opening and the presentation of a Royal Charter giving it a new constitution.

Adults who dealt with Shirley were not always so charmed. The teaching staff knew that he considered them expendable. One housemaster in 1935 describes 'the glorious uncertainty of employment at the King's School in those pioneering days. It was like a protracted game of snakes and ladders, with the snakes outnumbering the ladders. None of us entered the Mint Yard at the beginning of term without finding someone with exciting news. A gardener, a waiter or a boy would be there to tell us, in confidence, that we were no longer living where we thought, that there was a new master to take over part of our job or that we had been sending too many articles to the laundry'. But in a school which soon grew to three times its previous size the masters were as important to the boys as even such a headmaster as Shirley. As at any school there were good, bad and ridiculable. Among the ridiculable was the Revd A. D. R. Brooke, in shape a latter-day Tar Mason, described as 'a sort of Friar Tuck but not as jolly'. 'Because he was so

Above: The move to Cornwall was fully vindicated when Canterbury was bombed on 1 June 1942, allegedly in retaliation for the bombing of Cologne: the morning after the raid.

Left: King George VI, Queen Elizabeth and Princess Elizabeth listen to a Latin speech of welcome by the Captain of School. The King replied in English and presented his Royal Charter to the School (11 July 1946).

fat,' says Michael Mayne, 'we called him the Tank. . . . The challenge was to steal his cassock belt and see how many standard-sized boys could fit inside it. Was it nine?' Among the good was Geoffrey Lampe, who, as an army chaplain in Normandy, finding himself in the same slit trench as an old boy, observed, 'Malory, I don't think we have met since the Peloponnesian War'. Lampe became Regius Professor of Divinity at Cambridge. Admired, too, for their scholarship and as men, were Roach (classics and modern languages) who became a headmaster at Hull, and Mitchell (history).

With the Dean and Chapter Shirley was equally ruthless in getting his way, playing on their personalities, forming and dissolving alliances, opposing or flattering, frank or petulant as necessary. He could also support some course of action for no other reason than that it was the good thing to do. One boy remembers finding him in the ancient outdoor lavatories, damaging them with a hammer, so that he could have them declared a health risk and force the Chapter to replace them.

He had a celebrated difference with the best known of all the school's governors, Field Marshal Montgomery. As a boy Montgomery had spent a term at the Junior School, and he had continued to take an interest in the school, making what in retrospect seems an astonishing two-day visit to lecture to it in Cornwall not long before D-day. After the war he became a governor, but had by this time ceased to believe that public schools had a future, and when Shirley reached retiring age, pressed him to resign. Shirley did not resign, and soon afterwards, when Montgomery failed to attend the required number of consecutive governors' meetings, got him removed.

Shirley also manœuvred against Dr Hewlett Johnson, the Red Dean. Though he was genuinely grateful for the support the dean had given him in his early years, he was concerned at the effect on the school's reputation of having for chairman of its Governing Body someone with such left-wing views. He also recognized in the dean someone who was a match for him, and knew that he would get

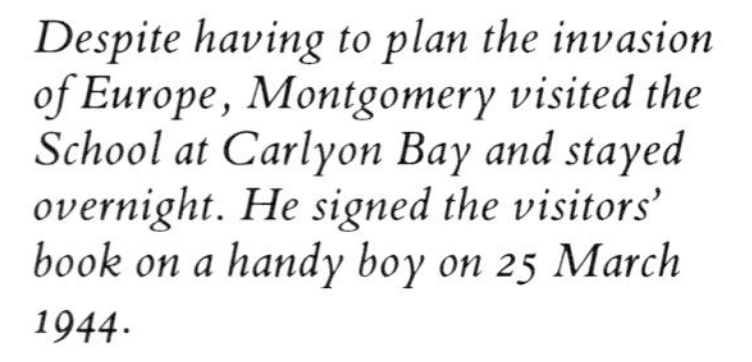
Despite having to plan the invasion of Europe, Montgomery visited the School at Carlyon Bay and stayed overnight. He signed the visitors' book on a handy boy on 25 March 1944.

his way with the Governing Body and the Chapter more easily if he could isolate the dean. For both reasons he was willing to sign the letter he and the other canons wrote to *The Times* in 1940 dissociating themselves from the dean's political views. In 1956, when the dean supported the Russian invasion of Hungary, and showed the Russian leader, Malenkov, round the cathedral during Evensong, Shirley put the Deanery out of bounds, and the Governing Body voted that the dean should cease to take the chair at their meetings.

The boys were divided about the dean. James Hamilton-Paterson remembers him as extremely kind. He would be invited to tea with him and asked for advice about what records the dean should give his daughter for her birthday. But one year the dean 'put up a huge blue and white banner across the front of the Deanery which read "Christians Ban Nuclear Weapons". On Guy Fawkes Night one couldn't say the school was actively encouraged to attack the Deanery; but nobody did anything to prevent a barrage of rockets etc [being] fired directly at the building, some of which did actual damage and broke windows . . .'.

With one adult Shirley achieved an unexpectedly friendly and mutually beneficial relationship: Somerset Maugham. When he arrived at Canterbury, Shirley was assured that Maugham hated the school and the school, as represented by the O.K.S. Association, would never forgive Maugham for *Of Human Bondage*. Shirley suggested to Maugham that all schools of the 1880s had been 'more or less as barbarous', and in the autumn of 1936 persuaded him to make the first of many visits to the school.

Dr. Hewlett Johnson, the Red Dean. (Punch cartoon by Ronald Searle, 1957.)

Somerset Maugham's ashes were buried in the School grounds, in accordance with his wish, on 22 December 1965. This gate with his symbol leads to the burial place.

The respective benefits they brought each other are symbolized by the story of Maugham's ashes and the school boathouse. In oriental style, without anything formal being said, they agreed that each would help the other, Maugham with £3000 (three-quarters of the cost) of the boathouse, Shirley by arranging for Maugham's ashes to be buried in the Precincts. They helped each other in more fundamental ways. By his many other gifts (the Maugham Library, a physics laboratory, his manuscripts), and above all by associating himself with the school, Maugham made an important contribution to the prestige which Shirley so badly wanted for it. By receiving Maugham and his gifts, Shirley gave him 'a security here' – the phrase is Shirley's – which he needed.

Two of his staff on whom Shirley relied heavily were his secretary, Miss Milward, who had come with him from Worksop, and his steward, Harry Curtis. The Curtis family served the school for 100 years – it was Harry's mother who, as parlour-maid, had rescued Blore from Canterbury High Street. In the 1920s and 30s Curtis became butler to Latter and then Birley, and Shirley instantly promoted him to steward, observing characteristically, 'You're supposed to be one of the few here with any brains. What ideas have you?'. For over 30 more years Curtis contributed his brains and ideas to the school's administration. It was he who, in the terms of the time, provided the logistical support for the Cornish evacuation. 'I did most of my er, work', he said when he retired, 'in the General Wolfe at St Austell.' He referred not, of course, to drinking but to foraging.

Shirley's grand final project was the hall which is named after him. For this he raised £70 000 of the £90 000 which it cost. Architecturally the hall cannot be admired. It jars with its surrounding without being adventurous in compensation. But it supplies a much needed assembly hall, and makes a fine concert hall with good acoustics.

One of his rare failures was his attempt to revive the school's Feast Society, and raise for the school an endowment of £100 000. In July 1939 a great banquet was held to re-launch the society and its appeal, with the Duke of Kent there as its president. It was not Shirley's fault that two months later the war began and two years later the duke was killed in an air crash. The society never met again and its appeal foundered.

One of his great successes was the starting of King's Week. In 1951 several circumstances combined to give him the opportunity: in particular, the decline of the pre-war Festival which the cathedral had supported, and the Festival of Britain. One of its great advantages, Shirley saw, would be to keep the school together during the second half of the summer term, an increasing problem as final examinations were set earlier and earlier. Today King's Week has become a remarkable demonstration of the school's talents, especially in music and drama, with four concerts, and at least as many plays, as well as exhibitions and many other fringe activities – indeed it can well claim to be the school-world's Edinburgh Festival.

In his 1961 pre-retirement report to the governors, Shirley, never a modest man but nor a dishonest one, listed his achievements during his 27 years at the school. Its numbers had risen to between 600 and 700; it had obtained 260 scholarships or exhibitions to Oxford or Cambridge, compared with 26 in the previous 20 years; in music 'no school is comparable'; its annual income was £295 000, compared to £22 719 in 1935; it had no debts and had spent £400 000 on new buildings or modernizing older ones. On Shirley's final Speech Day the Captain of the School, Michael Morpurgo, said that the King's School had in effect had three foundations: 'once so long ago that the founder's name is obscure, once by Henry VIII, and finally, its greatest foundation, by Fred'. He did not exaggerate.

An Extraordinary Headmaster was the title given to the biography of Shirley by D. L. Edwards. 'To follow an Extraordinary Headmaster', said Canon J. P. Newell, summing up his 13 years as Shirley's successor, 'was a lesson among other things in humility. If all goes on superbly well it is assumed that it does so by some process of predestined automation. If it doesn't there is only one person to blame.' Newell understood that merely to preside over a period without change was not wise or useful. One of his aims was to give the school an administrative structure which would run it effectively, without the continual interference – however inspiring – of the headmaster. In retrospect Shirley's regime seemed to have been one of continual improvisation with Shirley as the prime improviser. Shirley's account, quoted above, of the school's evacuation to Cornwall shows how happy he was in that role.

Newell also worked to improve the school's accommodation which, in spite of Shirley's improvements, he saw as 'woeful', spending on this and other buildings over half a million pounds. A new sanatorium and St Mary's Hall were the most important additions. And he at least maintained the school's academic standing. In pursuit of delegation, he expanded the excellent historian R. W. Harris's responsibility for the curriculum, who resisted fancy changes – even if he also gave it a bias towards his own subject. Newell presided over another development which was to turn out as significant for the school's future as any of Shirley's: the cautious introduction of girls into the Sixth Form.

Above: The Great Hall to its builder, Canon Shirley, but renamed the Shirley Hall in his honour when he retired in 1962.

Below: The Queen Mother and Canon Shirley on 12 July 1962.

He was headmaster through what may be called Flower-folk time, a period when – as he put it more prosaically – there was 'a swing from the authoritarianism of the past'. It was then that he admits to having felt like the Dutch boy with his finger in the hole of the dyke wall. Others saw him as reassuringly firm and stern. 'He had a very clear image of what a Headmaster should look like', Dean Ian White-Thomson writes in his obituary, ' – and he looked like one; he had a clear image of how a Headmaster should dress – and he dressed like one, in gown, mortar-board and bands. If there had not been such a word as meticulous someone would have had to invent it to describe Peter.' Peter was a name Newell had given himself. He was christened John Philip, but the boys, significantly, called him 'The Pont', derived from Pontiff.

One boy, David Hopkins, remembers him as 'a tall imposing figure dressed in a grey suit, clerical collar, black gown and mortar-board, standing in the Green Court in front of the office. There he would be every morning after assembly to see boys and staff, to criticise, to congratulate, or simply to deal with day to day routine. On windy days the gown would flutter and the hand would frequently reach to the head to ensure that the mortar-board was still in proper place.' The description points to Newell's most serious failing. However much he aimed to give the running of the school to others, he was still visibly central, the captain of his ship on its windswept bridge.

Flower-child, 1972. (Punch cartoon by 'Smilby', June 1972.)

To put it at its most severe, he tried to replace Shirley's unscrupulous charm with a more dignified formality, but as a result sacrificed Shirley's ability to inspire. This was not for want of trying. He is said to have known the names of all 700 boys and girls in the school. He took a particular interest in those who were backward or in trouble. Typically he chose to mention one of these in his farewell speech, a talented Rugby three-quarter who was so unacademic that he even failed to pass into the army, but who returned from his interview at Westbury 'with the Brigadier's daughter'.

The final verdict on Newell must be that he carried out the impossible task of succeeding Shirley competently, giving the school the chance to pause for breath which it needed. But he never successfully coped with the King's School's special problem of co-operating with the Dean and Chapter. Nor was he a natural headmaster – in retirement as the parson of Goudhurst he became relaxed and expansive. As an amateur actor his set piece was a parody of Noel Coward in *Private Lives*.

Canon J. P. Newell, oil by Anna Zinkeisen, 1973.

'We have a surprise for you', Canon Derek Ingram Hill remembers being told at the time of the appointment of Newell's successor. 'It's another clergyman.' After two clerics in a row, the Governing Body had set out to find a layman, but Canon Peter Pilkington's qualities had made them change their minds.

Pilkington was in most ways a contrast to Newell. He was notably short and slight where Newell was tall, and informal where Newell was dignified. More significantly, they had different backgrounds. Newell had been headmaster of Bradford Grammar School, a northern day school. Pilkington, brought up in County Durham, had after Cambridge been a curate in Bakewell, Derbyshire, and a teacher in Africa. But his most recent position, indeed his only English teaching experience, had been Master in College at Eton. Pilkington's Eton experiences are essential in understanding his achievements at the King's School. Again and

Opposite: King's Week.

Peter Pilkington experimenting with one of the computers he introduced to the School.

again he can be seen to have used Eton as the model for his reforms. Centrally, he considered that the King's School lacked 'style', and his conception of style was inevitably Etonian.

Pilkington and Newell, however, faced similar problems. It may seem surprising after the real achievements of their predecessors that each saw the school's accommodation as deplorable. But on each occasion the standards of competing schools (not to mention the expectations of parents) had risen and those of the King's School had not kept pace. To Pilkington the various outhouses in the town seemed particularly 'squalid', and Luxmoore House had the added disadvantage that it was 20 minutes' walk from the Mint Yard.

Pilkington's pre-eminently stylish expansion of the school's premises was the occupation of St Augustine's. The story of how the school might have acquired the abbey's ruins in 1834 has been told (see page 61). The Anglican missionary college which instead opened there in 1848 functioned until 1942. After the Second World War the buildings were used to provide Anglican clergy with sabbatical years until 1969, then by King's College, London, as a finishing school for men about to be ordained. But by the mid-1970s King's College had relinquished them and the trustees were looking for ways to dispose of their property. Pilkington had discovered this before he came to Canterbury. He also knew that the new university and Christ Church teachers' training college both wanted the abbey. There followed, in his own words, 'quite a battle', but one which, by determination and skill, with the help of one of the trustees, Canon Robinson, he won. Diplomacy of this sort was Pilkington's forte and it was perhaps because he found exercising his skill so enjoyable that he was so often successful.

The two houses he opened in the fine buildings which Butterfield had designed for the missionary college were named after the old King's Scholars, John Tradescant, seventeenth-century royal gardener, and William Broughton, first Bishop of Australia. St Augustine's has become, as Pilkington intended, 'the school's flagship'.

Expansion on such a grand scale needed money – the school did so anyway – Newell had left it £60 000 in debt. Its 'squalid outhouses' provided a great part of what was necessary. Unlike the Precincts buildings, they were its property. By selling them and their land Pilkington also obtained the money he needed for a general upgrading of the school's houses, and for two new houses – a replaced Luxmoore and Mitchinson's.

Architect's elevations for these were sent to, among others, the distinguished old boy and writer, Patrick Leigh Fermor. Though Leigh Fermor by then considered himself forgiven, his school career had ended abruptly when he was found in the arms of a local greengrocer's daughter. The greengrocer, according to legend, had five of these, and would show a notice in his window reading 'Kentish cherries, ripe and ready'. About the design for Mitchinson's, which was to occupy the site in the Mint Yard where the old Almonry had stood, Leigh Fermor wrote that it suggested 'a hybrid between a prefab, a garage and a potting shed'. The materials to be used might be 'cut stone and rose-red tiles half as old as time, but the style and feeling convey pebbledash, hardboard and planks painted with creosote, with a perfunctory nod towards Anne Hathaway from the gables'. He submitted his own suggestions in Norman, Renaissance, Tudor, and Georgian styles, but unfortunately all would have been hugely expensive.

The design for the other new house, Luxmoore, was less controversial, incorporating mediaeval remains on the site into a pleasing modern building. But the really important feature of both houses was that Pilkington managed, with the support of Dean Victor de Waal and the Chapter, to have them both built within the Precincts – something which had not been thought possible until McGuire and Murray, architects with a national reputation, took a fresh outside look at the problem. The whole school was thus concentrated around the cathedral.

Inside these houses, and in those he refurbished, Pilkington introduced a change which he considered equally important by abolishing the traditional 'hall'. This, he considered, saddled boys with unhelpful roles – 'bully', 'swot'. Instead he created Eton-style studies where, in the words of the second master at the time, 'adolescent love of squalor and nest-building could be given rein'.

If the school's living accommodation was now concentrated, some of its other needs had to be met by outward expansions. The three most important of these

On 24 June 1981 the Queen Mother paid her fourth visit to King's. She opened the new Luxmoore House and inaugurated Mitchinson's – two major Pilkington developments.

The name plaque of Mitchinson's, carved by Ralph Beyer in 1981.

were the acquiring of the Old Synagogue for a music recital hall, the building of a craft and design centre, and the establishment of the art department in the thirteenth-century Blackfriars.

With St Augustine's had come Bailey House, which made possible another reform: the rehousing of the school's girls. Until then many had lived dispersed in digs around the Precincts. Pilkington also systematized the hitherto *ad hoc* admission of girls, initiated by Newell, by establishing examinations for places and scholarships. Against opposition from traditionalists who foresaw 'problems with fielding teams', he allowed the number of girls to increase till they formed a third of the Sixth Form. Even for this greater number of places there was much competition, with the result that only girls of a high standard were admitted and standards in many activities – though not football and cricket – rose.

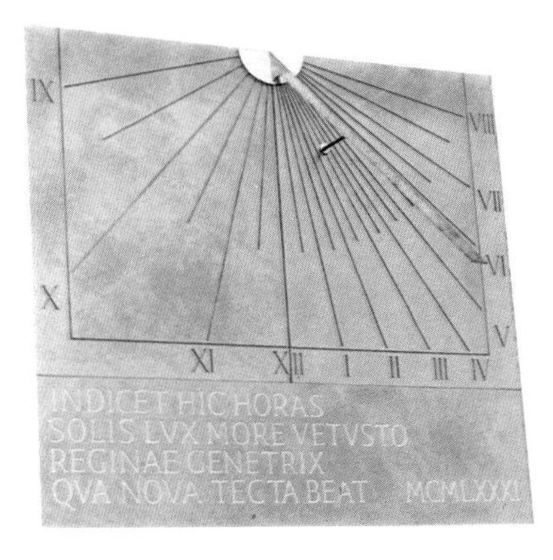

The sundial marking the opening of the new Luxmoore in the Precincts. The Latin verse contains a play of words on the name Luxmoore.

While it is surprising – but understandable – that Newell had let the school's accommodation fall behindhand it is more so that he had failed to systematize its administration, since he had clearly understood that this was needed. Again Eton was the model for the school committees which Pilkington established. Today the housemasters' committee, senior teachers' committee, the budget committee and others discuss and give advice about the aspects of the school which concern them, not only influencing the way it develops, but forming an organizational network which effectively manages the school.

Right at the start, as a signal that there would be changes, Pilkington had reformed the school's cathedral attendances. For every second Sunday Matins service he substituted a choice between communion service and (for the Sixth Form) a talk by a visitor, or (for junior boys) a service particularly addressed to them. He also at once relaxed the school's dress regulations, allowing boys to wear plain clothes at certain times. Again Eton was his model, and every boy might have been expected to welcome such liberalization, but some did not, and printed cards were left about reading 'We do not want to be eaten'.

The incident is a clue to Pilkington's most serious weakness: he was never on easy terms with the boys of the school, so much so that a dayboy claims not to have known what he looked like till he came to say goodbye (he must have had his eyes shut during a great many sermons). One night Pilkington forgot his key and was forced to climb the Precincts wall. Dusting himself down in the flowerbed, he was surprised by a heavy thump as a boy landed beside him. 'I didn't expect you here, sir,' the boy said. 'I am ubiquitous,' Pilkington replied. It was an apt description. Pilkington was indeed present in all that happened, but to the boys often invisibly. Pilkington's weakness is particularly surprising since one of his reforms was designed to humanize housemasters by insisting that they all had accommodation which would be sufficient for a wife and children.

The opposite is true about his relationships with almost all adults. Barbara Slimming, secretary both to Newell and Pilkington (and an admirer of both men) remembers that she would be able to tell Pilkington if she wanted 'don't be silly, you can't do that', something she could never have said to Newell. While Newell would dictate to her all his letters, Pilkington would trust her to write the sort of standard letters routine correspondence required. While Newell would hesitate, Pilkington would want everything done five minutes before he'd thought of it.

Opposite: The rising moon over the Great Gate of St Augustine's.

Pilkington's easy friendliness was especially important in forming excellent relationships with Dean de Waal and the other cathedral canons, who still formed the Chapter with its rights over most of the school's buildings, and who remained an important part of the Governing Body. Individually they became some of the many friends he made in the Precincts. If he needed to come to them in committee with his school's problems, they would come to him with personal ones.

Pilkington's wife Helen must be mentioned, indeed so should Newell's and Shirley's. It had been one of Latter's disadvantages that he was a bachelor, so innocent about some aspects of marriage that he did not realise his housemaid was pregnant until she gave birth in his bathroom. The last three headmasters' wives have in their different ways played such invaluable roles that it is difficult to imagine their husbands without them. In her husband's lifetime, possibly by choice as much as by necessity, Mrs Shirley was a background figure providing stateliness – she had private means. She allowed some of her warmth to show when small boys came to their house. It was really only after his death that she emerged as a Precincts personality in her own right, a grande dame with a sharp eye and a sense of fun. Quiet loyalty was Mary Newell's essential quality. She supported someone who was essentially shy, disliked going anywhere without her and always wanted to sit by her at a meal. Helen Pilkington – also well-to-do in her own right – was a woman of much style. An excellent cook from whom many learned about hospitality, she played a central part in Pilkington's much expanded entertaining.

Helen Pilkington and other King's School ladies compiled this excellent and very practical book, and John Ward drew the illustrations, for the Appeal of 1980.

Together they bought a fine Somerset house, often lending it to masters or other Canterbury friends.

If Shirley was a more flamboyant headmaster than Pilkington, with a greater flair for publicity, when the facts are considered objectively, Pilkington built or acquired more new premises for the school. The importance of his concentration of the school round the cathedral and St Augustine's cannot be exaggerated. And of more permanent value than Shirley's inspirational personal leadership were Pilkington's decentralising reforms. At their most basic they meant that to get something done in the school it was no longer necessary to catch the headmaster in a good mood. Shirley left behind him an enormously exciting community but something of a rogue elephant among schools. The school that Pilkington left was, in the words of the present headmaster, 'comfortably established among the leading schools of the country'.

Working together.

This necessarily meant that in 1986 Canon Anthony Phillips had the difficult inheritance of a school at a high point in its history. He has not rested on this peak. The introduction of full co-education to the school will certainly be seen as the most important event of his headmastership. Pilkington had already greatly increased the number of girls. From 1990 they have been able to enter at thirteen years old and will ultimately make up as high a proportion of the school as their entrance-exam results earn them. Important too has been the strengthening of the tutorial system. Pastoral care of the individual is very much the King's ethos.

Chief among building achievements will come the magnificent new sports centre, costing £2½ million, for which the foundation stone was laid in 1990. This

The first intake of thirteen-year-old girls in September 1990 aroused considerable public interest. The Headmaster, Canon Anthony Phillips, poses with some new arrivals for the press.

gap in the school's facilities will finally be plugged – ironically by someone who would never claim to be a sportsman.

If in these ways Canon Anthony Phillips's influence on the school must surely in future come to be at the very least mentionable alongside that of Pilkington, in another he has overcome Pilkington's one weakness: easy rapport between the boys and girls and the headmaster. Describing himself as an extrovert, he is ready at all times to meet and talk to them informally – behaviour natural to him, but also doubtless confirmed by his time as Chaplain and Fellow of St John's College, Oxford. He and his wife visit each boy or girl regularly in their rooms, besides entertaining many of them at their home.

Two anniversaries approach – the 450th of Henry VIII's statutes in 1991, and the 1400th of the original Augustinian foundation in 1997. Independent schools will never be without financial or political problems, but it will be some very unexpected ones which prevent the King's School from celebrating these events in fine shape, under the sort of leadership it deserves.

CHRONOLOGY

CHRONOLOGICAL LIST OF HEADMASTERS

The date is the date of appointment or of occurrence of the name in a document.
There is continuity unless stated or implied otherwise.

1259 Master Robert
1292 Master Nicholas occurs
1306 Robert of Maidstone
1310 John Everard
1321 Ralph of Waltham occurs
1348 Walter occurs
1360 Walter Haye occurs
1374 John Bocton appointed by Prior Gillingham but replaced by John of Langham by Edward III
1376 Robert Reynell, MA
1421 John Syre, BA occurs
1437 John Colbroke occurs
1443 John Westhill
1445 Richard Waterton
1464 John Gedney occurs
c.1475 One 'who hath taught gramer att Wynchester and atte Seynt Antonyes in London' occurs
1502 Richard Church, BA
c.1524 John Twyne, BCL, New Inn Hall, Oxford continues from 1541 as headmaster of the King's School
1561 Revd Anthony Rushe, MA, Fellow of Magdalen College, Oxford
1565 Revd William Absolom, MA, Fellow of Corpus Christi College, Oxford
1566 John Gresshop, MA, Christ Church, Oxford
1580 Revd Nicholas Goldsborough, BD, MA, Queens' College, Cambridge and Corpus Christi College, Oxford
1584 Revd William Arnold, MA, Christ Church, Oxford
1584 Anthony Shorte, BCL, Fellow of All Souls College, Oxford
1591 Roger Raven, MA, Clare Hall, Cambridge
1615 Revd John Ludd, MA, Trinity College, Cambridge
1649 Edward Browne, MA
1659 Henry Montague, BA, Magdalen College, Oxford, expelled in 1660
1661 John Paris, MA, St. John's College, Cambridge
1665 Revd George Lovejoy, MA, Fellow of Merton College, Oxford
1684 Richard Johnson, BA, St. John's College, Cambridge
1689 Revd Thomas Atkins, MA, Trinity College, Cambridge
1700 Revd David Jones, MA, Magdalen Hall, Oxford
1713 Revd John Smith, MA, Corpus Christi College, Cambridge
1718 Revd George Smith, MA, Fellow of St. John's College, Oxford
1721 Revd John Le Hunt, MA, Fellow of King's College, Cambridge
1731 Revd John Frances, MA, Christ Church, Oxford
1734 Revd Richard Monins, MA, Fellow of St. John's College, Cambridge
1747 Revd Robert Talbot, MA, Fellow of Clare Hall, Cambridge
1750 Revd Osmund Beauvoir, MA, DD (Lambeth), FRS, Fellow of St. John's College, Cambridge
1782 Revd John Tucker, MA, Trinity College, Cambridge
1785 Revd Christopher Naylor, MA, St. John's College, Cambridge
1816 Revd John Birt, DD, Christ Church, Oxford
1832 Revd George Wallace, MA (Lambeth and Cantab), Trinity College, Cambridge
1859 Revd John Mitchinson, DD, DCL, Fellow of Pembroke College, Oxford
1873 Revd George John Blore, DD, Student of Christ Church, Oxford
1886 Revd Thomas Field DD, Fellow of Magdalen College, Oxford

1896 Revd Arthur John Galpin, DD, Trinity College, Oxford
1910 Revd Charles Robert Loraine McDowall, MA, Exeter College, Oxford
1916 Algernon Latter, MA, Trinity College, Oxford
1927 Norman Pellew Birley, DSO, MC, MA, New College, Oxford
1935 Revd Frederick Joseph John Shirley, DD, PhD, LLB, St. Edmund Hall, Oxford, and London
1962 Revd John Philip Peter Newell, MA, Magdalen College, Oxford
1975 Revd Peter Pilkington, MA, Jesus College, Cambridge
1986 Revd Anthony Charles Julian Phillips, BD, PhD, King's College, London, and Gonville and Caius College, Cambridge, Fellow of Trinity Hall, Cambridge, and of St. John's College, Oxford

CHRONOLOGICAL LIST OF LOWER MASTERS

The date is the date of appointment or of occurrence of the name in a document. There is continuity unless stated or implied otherwise.

1464 Thomas Hikson occurs
1542 William Wells, BA, Oxford, first 'Hypodidascalus' of the King's School
1553 John Shawe
1554 Saunders (perhaps John Saunders, BA, Magdalen College, Oxford)
1555 Thomas Paulyn
1561 Peter Levens, MA, Fellow of Magdalen College, Oxford
1563 Paul Colman
1564 Revd Matthew Bourne, MA, Fellow of Magdalen College, Oxford
1565 Edward Caldwell, BA, Christ Church, Oxford
1569 Revd George Elye, MA, Oxford
1571 Robert Rose, BA, Oxford
1585 Augustine Lake, BA, Christ Church, Oxford
1586 Revd Thomas Wilson, MA, Queen's College, Oxford
1587 Robert Brown
1588 Revd Thomas Constant, MA, Corpus Christi College, Cambridge
1591 Revd Rufus Rogers, MA, University College, Oxford
1610 Revd John Ludd, MA, Trinity College, Cambridge
1615 Revd Samuel Raven, MA, Sidney Sussex College, Cambridge
1633 Thomas Roberts, BA
1633 Edward Browne, MA
1649 John Croydon (died shortly before expulsion of 1660)
1661 Revd John Culling, BA, Clare College, Cambridge
1681 Richard Johnson, BA, St. John's College, Cambridge
1684 Revd John Booth, MA, Queens' College, Cambridge
1689 Revd Gilbert Burroughs, MA (perhaps Scottish)
1715 Revd William Burroughs, MA, Balliol College, Oxford
1723 Revd John Frances, MA, Christ Church, Oxford
1731 Revd James Evans, BA, Trinity College, Cambridge
1743 Revd William Gurney, MA, Corpus Christi College, Cambridge
1755 Revd John Tucker, MA, Trinity College, Cambridge
1776 Revd William Howdell, BA, St. John's College, Cambridge
1779 Revd John Tucker, MA, Trinity College, Cambridge (son of John Tucker above and later headmaster)
1782 Revd Christopher Naylor, MA, St. John's College, Cambridge
1785 Revd William Chafy, MA, Fellow of Sidney Sussex College, Cambridge
1786 Revd Edward William Whitaker, BA, Christ Church, Oxford
1787 Revd John Francis, MA, Pembroke College, Cambridge
1821 Revd William Pitman Jones, MA, Pembroke College, Oxford
1830 Revd George Wallace, MA (Lambeth and Cantab), Trinity College, Cambridge
1832 Anby Beatson, MA, Sidney Sussex College, Cambridge
1859 Thomas Streatfeild Lipscomb, MA, Pembroke College, Oxford
1871 Revd Richard Greaves Hodgson, MA, Christ Church, Oxford
1908 Revd Leonard Hugh Evans, MA, Pembroke College, Cambridge
1914 C. W. Bell, MA, Trinity College, Oxford (absent on service 1916–18)
1918 G. F. J. Rosenberg, MA, St. John's College, Cambridge
1925 William Nathaniel Goss, MA, Queen's College, Oxford
1933 Joseph Bastable Harris, MC, MA, Selwyn College, Cambridge (Mr Harris retired in July 1959 and there was no Lower Master for the next two terms)
1960 John Boyd Wilson, MA, New College, Oxford
1962 John Richard Elgar Paynter, MA, Sidney Sussex College, Cambridge
1976 Paul Gilson Wenley, MA, Corpus Christi College, Cambridge
1989 David Paul Humberstone, MA, PhD, Fitzwilliam College, Cambridge, and London

INDEX

Figures in italic refer to black and white illustrations. Figures in bold refer to colour illustrations

i
X